CHINESE & ORIENTAL ART

CHINESE & ORIENTAL ART

Chinese & Oriental Art

adapted by Michael Batterberry

Foreword by Howard Conant,
New York University

McGRAW-HILL BOOK COMPANY

New York • San Francisco • Toronto

Also in the Discovering Art Series:

NINETEENTH CENTURY ART adapted by Ariane Ruskin

Acknowledgment is hereby given to Purnell & Sons Ltd. for the right to base this work on the text of the magazine series "Discovering Art" and to Fratelli Fabbri Editori for the right to make adaptations from the Italian text of *Capolavori Nei Secoli.*

FOREWORD

by Howard Conant, *Professor and Chairman, Department of Art Education; and Head, Division of Creative Arts,*
New York University

THIS HANDSOME volume of Oriental art meets an immediate need in art education. Good books on the art of Asia are rarely found in most European and North American libraries. It is an area that libraries have either slighted or excluded entirely on grounds as weak as the idea that it belongs to another culture—not our own. Readers will therefore welcome this addition to the library lists. They will happily absorb the lavish splendor of its illustrations and the author's lucid commentary on the arts of China and other Asian countries.

The days of Kipling's "East is East and West is West and never the twain shall meet" are dead. The reader of today must know of the history and culture of the East. We are deeply involved even at this moment in the future of Asia. Readers demand to know more about the arts, culture, and history of the Orient, where some of the world's oldest civilizations exist and half of the world's population lives.

Mr. Michael Batterberry's *Chinese & Oriental Art* immediately establishes and maintains a profound insight and scholarly assurance. Many readers already assume that the arts of the East are as important as the arts of any other part of the world. Some readers, in fact, will probably respond more easily to the spiritual bases of Eastern art.

Chinese & Oriental Art should be welcomed and well-received by teachers of art and social studies and should certainly be included as a standard reference book in every school and community library. Mr. Batterberry's direct and easily comprehended, though never condescending, style together with more than three hundred and eighty magnificent illustrations readily qualify his book for use as a secondary school or college text. In the fields of art, history, and the humanities, it can readily serve as a reference volume for courses in literature, music, and religion.

Mr. Batterberry's history of Oriental art clearly and succinctly describes the gradual development of Asian culture from its earliest neolithic Chinese origins to the present day. He carefully traces the evolution of uniquely Oriental art modes from one dynasty or epoch to another. He reveals their relationships without erasing their subtly important differences. In the best tradition of art criticism, he clearly expresses aesthetic value judgments without once lapsing into dogmatic pronouncements. His obviously deep interest in and extensive knowledge of the arts of Asia show up in each sentence of this book.

CONTENTS

Early China

THE CHINESE, from the earliest awakenings of their civilization, sought spiritual perfection not only in their art but also through a mystical harmony within themselves and with nature. They stressed in their art the dignified qualities of serenity, of graceful balance, of things being in their proper place. They avoided confusion, conflict, and violent emotions at all cost. Unsettling or revolutionary experiments in the arts were never welcomed; and fineness and expressions of nobility and inner worth were demanded. It has been said quite rightly that Chinese art is ultimately "a way of being." To appreciate it as fully as possible we must keep in mind a commandment of the great philosopher, Confucius: "Raise yourself to the beautiful."

The history of China may be traced back to a neolithic people who inhabited the fertile Yellow River plain about three thousand years before the birth of Jesus Christ. In view of these ancient origins, it may reasonably be said that Chinese civilization, despite many violent political and religious changes over the centuries, is the world's most enduring, particularly as far as uninterrupted dedication to the arts is concerned.

Little is known of the earliest Chinese craftsmen or the society which produced them other than that they lived in pounded earth settlements in northern Honan, Shantung, and Kansu. They created fine pottery and, especially, handsome funeral vessels for food and other provisions for the dead. They were terrified of demons, and conversed with the spirits of their ancestors by interpreting the cracks made by heat on ox bones and tortoise shells. Their legends taught them to revere Shang-ti, the Lord on High, and to honor the "Five Rulers," mythological heroes who had taught their forefathers how to raise silk worms, catch fish, domesticate animals, plow, reap, and use the wheel for transportation and for "throwing" pottery. They also believed that the Five Rulers had saved their country by digging canals and building dikes to hold back the floodwaters that spilled annually from the great rivers.

The first example of Chinese neolithic (late Stone Age) pottery we have to examine is a red earthenware jar from I-chou in northeast Hopei; it has been dated by archaeologists at about 3000 B.C. (Plate 2). Extremely simple and unadorned, this hand-made and primitively fired container nevertheless has a kind of plump gracefulness which erases any sense of crude craftsmanship. Its more complicated refined descendants (2000 B.C.–1300 B.C.) may be seen in Plates 2, 3, and 4. The first, an earthenware vase from Ma-ch'ang in Kansu, is decorated with bold black geometrical designs and is made of fine, smooth clay. The second and third are from Pan-shan and Ma-ch'ang, respectively, in Kansu, which may be located in the upper left-hand corner of the map on page 9 (Plate 1). Painted with greenish black rhythmic swirls, checks, diamonds, and crisscrossing lines (which may or may not have secret symbolic meanings), these jars are the artistic equals of the best prehistoric pottery to be found anywhere in the world. The neolithic inhabitants of China were energetically productive potters and were the first to practice this art, in which China has remained supreme up until recent times. At the same time that this painted ware was being made in Kansu, smooth and shiny articles appeared in Shantung, which, although they ranged in color from ebony to misty gray, are known today as the famous Black Pottery. Among the most unusual

THE CHINESE DYNASTIES

Shang (or Shang-Yin)	1523 B.C.–1028 B.C.
Chou	1027 B.C.–221 B.C.
Warring States	481 B.C.–221 B.C.
Ch'in	221 B.C.–206 B.C.
Han	206 B.C.–A.D. 220
Three Kingdoms	A.D. 220–A.D. 265
Six Dynasties	A.D. 265–A.D. 589
Sui	A.D. 581–A.D. 618
T'ang	A.D. 618–A.D. 907
Five Dynasties	A.D. 907–A.D. 960
Sung	A.D. 960–A.D. 1279
Yüan	A.D. 1280–A.D. 1368
Ming	A.D. 1368–A.D. 1644
Ch'ing	A.D. 1644–A.D. 1912

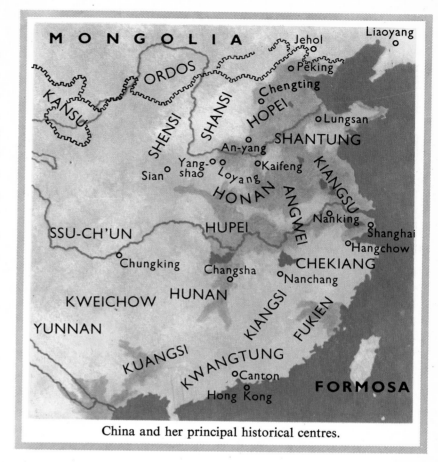

China and her principal historical centres.

1. Map of China's principal historical centers.

2. Red earthenware jar from I-chou in Hopei, northeast China (*c.* 3000 B.C.).

objects found in this group is the *li* tripod with its three hollow legs.

The Shang people, who enter history halfway through the second millennium B.C., also built with pounded earth and used animal bones in conversing with the spirits. They were great workers in jade, and they too had the *li* tripod. But whether this culture developed from the Black Pottery culture, or whether both were offshoots of an earlier one, is not clear.

Scholars now believe that the Shang, rulers of a loosely organized state, left their original home and moved somewhere to the north of Honan around 1500 B.C. They brought with them their religion, writing, and art. Their last capital was on the present site of An-yang, where it remained until the end of the dynasty, which in later years was called Shang-Yin.

The Shang dynasty (1523 B.C.–1028 B.C.), which saw the astonishing development of Chinese bronzes, established not only the *li* as a basic metallic shape or design, but also the *tsun,* the *ho,* the *kuang,* the *ting,* the *chia,* the *chüeh,* the *ku,* the *yu,* and other types of funeral vessels as well. These ancient bronzes lay in tombs thought to be legendary until this century, when they were dramatically discovered following excavations at An-yang and, more recently, Cheñg-chou. Among the thousands of different vessels found, it is possible to distinguish about forty basic shapes. Each type served a specific purpose in sacrificial or funeral ceremonies. Some were to contain wine or water, some were for storing food such as fruits, while still others were for cooking meat. They are known today as the "archaic bronzes," and their form and decoration

3. Painted earthenware jar from Pan-shan, Kansu (second millennium B.C.).

5. **Painted earthenware vase from Ma-ch'ang in Kansu, northwest China (*c.* 2000 B.C.).**

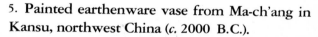

4. Painted earthenware vase from Ma-ch'ang, Kansu (1700–1300 B.C.).

display an extraordinary variety, originality, and richness of style. Their designs are uniformly beautiful. Notice how in (Plates 6–16) each the raised decoration or pattern somehow manages to suit perfectly the overall shape of the individual sacred object.

A difficult process of casting from molded

6. *Chia* type of bronze ritual vessel (Shang).

7. *Chih* type of bronze ritual vessel (Shang).

8. *Chüeh* type of bronze ritual vessel (Shang).

9. Covered *li* type of bronze ritual vessel (Shang).

10. *Tsun* type of bronze ritual vessel (Shang).

11. *Fang-i* type of container with square cover (Shang).

pieces of baked clay was used by the Shang craftsmen. Copper, alloyed with tin, to which lead was sometimes added, was the chief material employed in making bronze. The beautiful greenish surface of the archaic bronzes is due to a chemical reaction between the metal and earth or air and is only acquired with time. It is called "verdigris," or the "patina." Some of the major relics are shown in Plates 6 through 16. In addition, examples of stone sculpture, writing, wheel-made pottery, and carved jade were unearthed.

Probably the most fascinating specimen of the Shang bronzes is the *t'ao-t'ieh,* or earth demon, embracing and probably protecting a man (Plate 14). This particular *t'ao-t'ieh* was physically inspired by the tiger, an animal which has always been considered a protective force and good friend in Chinese folklore. The classic *t'ao-t'ieh* mask, used to ward off evil spirits, is usually missing its lower jaw, which makes the facial expression more terrifyingly ferocious.

To the Chinese, animals in art had symbolic meanings. Tigers symbolized the earth and power; birds represented the sun, air, and spiritual resurrection (as, for example, the owl in Plate 12). Snakes, because of their ability to shed their skins, suggested the never-ending renewal of Mother Earth, while the cicada, a species of cricket that lives its early days in larva form beneath the ground and then worms its way to the earth's surface to burst heavenward as a winged insect, symbolized spiritual afterlife. Domesticated animals were associated with a good and peaceful life. Upon close inspection it will be noticed that the tigerish *t'ao-t'ieh* figure in Plate 14 is itself decorated with animal forms—snakes, lizards, fish, buffalo, and ram horns. The deer peering between the *t'ao-t'ieh*'s ears is actually mounted on the lid of the funeral vessel.

Bronze was also used for the handle of a jade-bladed ceremonial dagger (Plate 16), the patina of the metal blurring into the green of China's most cherished stone.

Since ancient times the Chinese have carved jade into symbols of dignity and power—ornamental objects, parade arms—and into astronomical and musical instruments. A plaque probably punctured so that it could be worn as a medallion around an important person's neck (Plate 17) is an example. There is a common misconception that all jade must be green. On the contrary, it may be black, orange, brown, or cloudy white. Furthermore, it may be either opaque, like marble, or pale and semi-translucent, like an opal. Good jade is always smooth and cold to the touch. The Chinese believed that jade possessed a "magic virtue" and throughout their history fashioned from it such mysterious objects as the *pi* (Plate 18), a disc with a hole in the center, traditionally symbolizing heaven and imperial power, and the *ts'ung,* a rectangular tube adorned with a complicated series of notches, which some scholars say represents either Mother Earth or the empress. Others claim it to be some sort of astronomical device. The *ts'ung* in Plate 19 is carved in brilliant orange-amber jade.

The Shang dynasty has left sculpture as original as its bronzes, although none of the large statues have survived, and Shang art in general is infinitely varied and always of the same distinction and vigor. The importance of the excavations, which were undertaken only about thirty-five years ago, cannot be overemphasized. For, who otherwise would have believed in the slumbering existence of an ancient culture so rich that it had actually created stone sculpture, wheel-made pottery, carved jade, and bronzes which have never been surpassed?

In 1027 B.C. the warlike and hardy Chou

12. *Tsun* type of bronze ritual vessel with lid, in form of owl (Shang).

15. Bronze *ho* vessel with spout, lid, and *t'ao-t'ieh* mask (Shang).

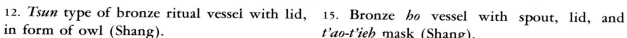

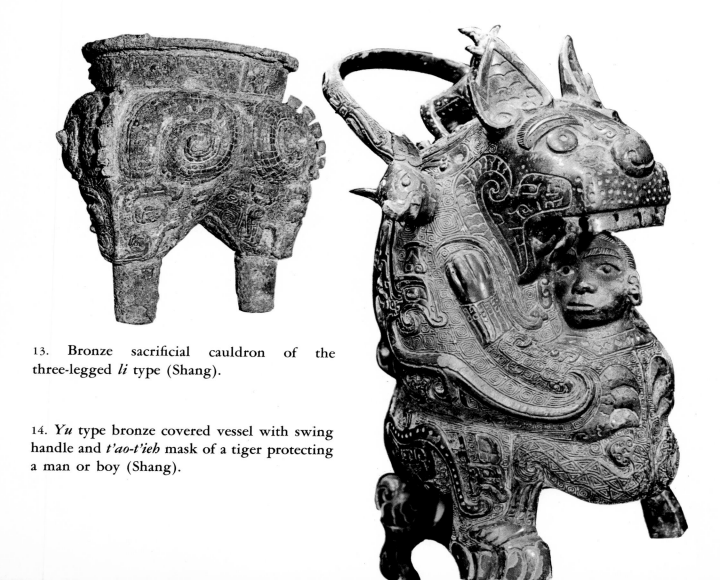

13. Bronze sacrificial cauldron of the three-legged *li* type (Shang).

14. *Yu* type bronze covered vessel with swing handle and *t'ao-t'ieh* mask of a tiger protecting a man or boy (Shang).

13

16. Ritual dagger with jade blade and bronze handle, from An-yang (Shang).

19. Jade *ts'ung* from An-yang (Shang).

17. Perforated green jade plaque (predynastic).

18. Jade *pi* disc (Chou).

stormed out of their western frontier land of Shensi in their glinting war chariots and conquered the peace-loving agricultural peoples of the An-yang district. The Shang ruler killed himself. The new militaristic masters proceeded to set up their own form of government based on a familial feudal system. Territories were parceled out to relatives, who immediately installed local garrisons of soldiers to ensure their lasting power.

While the Chou replaced the Shang dynasty with their own, they remained in their native Shensi until 770 B.C. They then moved their capital to Lo-yang in Honan, where it remained until the Chou's disappearance around 221 B.C.

The victory of the Chou over the Shang brought about a slowing down in the progress of art. Ritual bronze vases imitated Shang types for some time, but gradually new shapes and themes replaced them.

The military elegance of the Chou can be imagined on studying the bronze spiral finial with dragon's head in Plate 20. This impressive ornament was originally fitted to the end of a chariot pole. Except for this flair for military display, the Chou brought little else with them of artistic value. However, they were sensible enough to employ and encourage talented craftsmen of the old Shang school. Over the long years, bronze funeral vessels lost their original symbolic importance and the fear of demons almost entirely disappeared. Nevertheless, great respect was still paid to the dead, who were now buried in high funeral mounds rather than underground, as they had been previously. Traditional Shang forms were adopted for religious articles: Plate 21 shows a bronze *yu,* a covered pot with a swinging handle, used for liquids in religious rituals; Plate 22, a bronze wine vase of the *hu* type; Plate 23, a ceremonial *chung* bell. This

curiously shaped, studded bell has no clapper; it was slung from a ring on the handle and struck on its broad lower part with a wooden mallet.

Animals continued to figure prominently in Chinese art. The bronze *tsun*-type vessel

20. **Bronze spiral finial with dragon's head (Chou).**

22. Bronze vase of the *hu* type (Chou).

23. Ceremonial *chung* bell (Chou).

24. Bronze animal-shaped *tsun* (Chou).

in Plate 24 fancifully joins two rams back to back to form a symmetrical body. Traced onto the surface of the hollow spout between the two simply modeled heads is a Chou version of a *t'ao-t'ieh* mask with two dark circles suggesting the eyes. The *t'ao-t'ieh* has lost all its terrifying powers and

becomes merely a decorative motif. The tense, aggressive, and harshly carved tiger in Plate 25, ears erect, eyes bulging, teeth ferociously extended, manages to carry on a forceful tradition, however. The tiger's stripes cunningly disguise a lid, for the bronze figure is actually of the *tsun* category and was meant to hold wine.

Elephants, rhinoceroses, and other such unexpected animals lived in the ancient An-yang district. Many of their bones have been unearthed, and it is the scientific conclusion of archaeologists that the climate there was very warm (and hence suitable for such animals) before undergoing a violent change about one thousand years before Christ. The sturdy little bronze horse in Plate 26, which seems to be listening for a call from its master, was modeled after a breed of horses from the Mongolian steppes known for their long bodies, short legs, and tiny hooves. Dragons, the most famous of Chinese legendary creatures, are arranged in an amusing family group on the lid of the bronze brazier in Plate 27; a more natural horned head adorns the handle of the bronze *yu* in Plate 28. It is estimated that most of them were made in the third century B.C.

Man first appeared in religious or funeral art at the time of the Chou, and there is a simple and terrible reason why this is so: human sacrifice had been enthusiastically practiced until then. Shang graves have revealed hundreds of human skeletons. Along with them lie horses, chariots, and other favorite possessions of the dead. With the collapse of old superstitions, figurines were fortunately permitted to be buried in the place of actual live people. One of the very earliest to be discovered is the somewhat crude bronze kneeling man shown in Plate 29. This "funerary figure" has been dated at about 770 B.C. Far more touching, when we think what might have been their earlier fates, are the appealing little slave girl minding her master's doves and the lively acrobat performing a trick with a balancing bear cub in Plates 30 and 31. The doll-like funerary figures from Chang-sha (Plate 32), which are thought to have been buried between the sixth and third centuries B.C., are noticeably less refined than the bronze animals of the third century B.C. With their long primitive bodies, grotesque and floppy pegged-on hands, and pinched, painted smiles, these strange figures, who were supposed to come to life in the spirit world, look as if they were made by some entirely separate and limited culture.

Ordos is the name given to the semidesert region in north China; its pastoral, nomadic people influenced Chinese art and jewelry for a thousand years, starting in the fifth century B.C. They made bronze objects, usually small, for personal wear and as decorations for their horses' harnesses. They had, as well, knives and short swords ornamented in the "animal style" so popular with nomadic tribes in that general part of the world. Two of the oldest and most common motifs appear in Plates 33 and 34: the "preying animal" and the scene of "animal combat"—the tiger is slaying a deer, and the crocodilelike beast and the ram struggle together in a fight to the death. A bronze Ordos scabbard with a tiger and dragon snarling at each other across a human mask is seen in Plate 35, and a bronze deer, possibly a badge or standard carried on a pole, is shown in Plate 36.

By the time of the late Chou dynasty, the art of jade carving had reached a perfection never known before. Designs became fantastic and detailed. Compare the amazingly precise and lacy pattern, inspired by dragons,

25. **Bronze *tsun*-type container in the form of a tiger (Chou).**

which is carved into the ancient symbolic *pi* disk in Plate 37 with the decoration of the *pi* disk in Plate 18. The *pi* in Plate 38 boasts not only elaborately carved dragons on its rim but also an unusual surface looking as though it is studded with pin heads. This form of decoration was extremely difficult to achieve. The Chinese called the decoration "rice grain patterns." Like the *t'ao-t'ieh,* the *pi* had become more ornamental than mysterious. Besides these, a quantity of small jade statuettes, pins, pendants, and animal brooches has been found in

29. Bronze funerary figure of kneeling man (Chou).

26. Bronze horse (Late Chou).

27. Bronze brazier with large and small dragons (Late Chou).

28. Bronze *yu* with cover and swinging handle (Early Chou).

18

30. Bronze statuette of little slave girl with jade doves (Late Chou).

31. Bronze acrobat with balancing bear (Chou).

32. Painted wooden funerary figures (Late Chou).

19

33. Preying bronze tiger (Art of Ordos, Late Chou).

tombs. These were attached to the robe or sash of the dead—or the living—to give him magical protection. The jade fish and stag in Plate 39 are two examples of such ornaments.

Chou ceramics, like a number of their bronzes, loosely followed many of the Shang shapes. The clay owl in Plate 40 has none of the bold strength of the Shang bronze owl (Plate 12) in its outlines; nevertheless the brightly soft colors and cleverly simple design are lovely; indeed, in this case painting has almost completely taken the place of modeling. The ceramic bowl with cover in Plate 41, the covered pottery vase in Plate 42, and the brown-glazed stoneware bowl with lid in Plate 43 show three variations on the typically solid yet graceful Chou approach to design: The first imitates a bronze *tou*. The second is more intriguing, as decorative glass beads, now much worn down, for the first time have been pressed into the body of a vase. The third has a plain but handsome design incised on its lid and broad lip.

34. Bronze ornament of animal combat (Art of Ordos).

35. Bronze scabbard (Art of Ordos, Han).

36. Bronze deer (Art of Ordos).

37. Elaborate jade *pi* disc (Late Chou).

40. Painted clay vase in form of owl (Chou).

38. Jade *pi* with dragons (Late Chou).

39. Jade fish and stag (Late Chou).

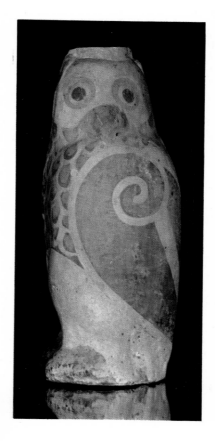

We come now to yet another great classic Chinese art form—lacquer, which was first used in the Chou dynasty. Lacquer is made of a tree sap, a natural resin, to which are added coloring substances. It can then be applied like varnish or paint to ceramics, wood, metal, or even materials like canvas. Certainly its most frequent application is to wood: First the wooden surface is smoothed down until it feels like glass; then the first layer of lacquer is spread on, followed by the second, the third, the fourth, and so on. If the lacquer is to be painted, there will probably be twenty to thirty layers; but if it is to be carved, there may be as many as two to three hundred. Furthermore, the craftsman-artist must wait until

41. Ceramic bowl with cover, of *tou* type (Chou).

44. Round box in lacquered wood (Chou).

42. Pottery vase and cover with glass bead insets (Chou).

45. Head of a beast in lacquered wood (Chou).

43. Brown-glazed stoneware bowl and lid (Chou).

46. Bronze urn of the *tou* type (Chou).

each coat has hardened thoroughly before laying on the next one. When this is finished, the much more painstaking work of carving begins. With a sharp little v-shaped knife, the artist, following a very complicated design, cautiously digs into the hardened lacquer, hairbreadth by hairbreadth. The slightest mistake can ruin the work of years. Sometimes, as we shall see in later periods, the work can become dizzyingly difficult, as in those cases where different-colored lacquers are piled up over each other, to be individually revealed by the delicate probing on different levels by the carver's knife. Examples of lacquer work are the red, black, and gold box in Plate 44 and the fantastic ibex head in Plate 45. Other elegant effects can be obtained by combining lacquer with layers of mother-of-pearl or semiprecious stones, or by mixing it with gold or silver powder.

47. Bronze *hu*-type vase with inlay (Late Chou).

The rise of the great feudal states, which led to the breakdown of Chou authority in 481 B.C., had a certain influence on the arts. Rivalry in wealth and ornate display went hand in hand with rivalry for power, and thereby created a demand for showy, luxurious art. During the Chou dynasty, gold was frequently combined with bronze in decorative patterns. Inscriptions found on bronze vessels show that they were now used for costly entertainments or as gifts from the king (whose official title had been elevated by the Chou to "Son of Heaven") or feudal lord. The bronze and gold *tou*-type container in Plate 46 and the *hu*-type vase decorated with five horizontal bands of golden prancing dragons (Plate 47) fall into this last category.

The Chou dynasty drew to an end in 221 B.C. Its last kings were sovereigns in name only. Their feudal states had become independent, and they fought each other for over two hundred years (481 B.C.–221 B.C.) even after the Chou dynasty had faded. Finally, the ruler of the state of Ch'in in the Wei valley, a tyrant who was to end his days in madness, massed his well-organized armies and brought the other states, one after the other, to heel. The old feudal system was swept away and replaced by a united centralized state with a civil service, standardized weights and measures, and, most important of all, a single, officially sanctioned, written language. In addition, this ruthless and efficient prince built a great frontier wall in the north (later to become part of the Great Wall) which linked his border fortresses in a strong line of defense against the Huns of the Mongolian steppes, meanwhile taking for himself the title "Shih Huang-ti," or "First Universal Emperor." He then added "Ch'in Shih" ("First of the Ch'in") to this impressive name; it is from this that the name China has been taken.

48. Pottery model of a house or watchtower from a tomb (Han).

When Ch'in Shih Huang-ti died as a madman in 210 B.C. (Kao, a blind lute player, had earlier failed to assassinate him), civil war broke out again.

An ignorant peasant general named Liu Pang defeated his rivals in the ensuing wars and made himself the first emperor of the Han dynasty as Han Kao-tsu. Despite his lowly origins, he admired and surrounded himself with educated people; basically kind and just, he managed to found a civilized and prosperous empire that was to last four hundred years. Trade flourished and walled towns sprang up all over the country.

We may gather some idea of the architecture of the dynasty from a ceramic model found in a Han tomb (Plate 48). The model is of a house or watchtower. This type of building had a wooden frame and might have two or more gaily decorated stories.

Even furniture design had become extremely imaginative. The fantastic baboon-faced monster blazing with silver and gold swirls (Plate 49) was a bronze table support of the late Chou or Warring States period. The charming gilt-bronze statuette of a clumsy little smiling bear (Plate 50) served

a similar purpose during the Han dynasty.

It is the tombs of the period, however, which most clearly indicate change and artistic progress. Beginning in the Chou period, the interior walls of the offering chambers, at the entrance of Chinese tombs, were usually lined with stone or clay slabs or tiles that were carved or stamped with pictures. The carved pictures (as in Plate 51) were drawn with deeply incised lines. In this way they stand out very clearly from the plain, putty-colored background, this style being similar to that used in much pottery decoration. Burial figures took many different forms. The strange massive creature (Plate 52), possibly a guardian, that

49. **Bronze table support (Late Chou or Warring States).**

50. **Gilt-bronze furniture support statuette of bear (Han).**

stood outside a Han tomb bears no relation to the painted wooden figurine of a woman (Plate 53) whose flowing sleeves are adorned with round glass ornaments much like those used in the Chou vase shown in Plate 42. This stiff figurine, in turn, has nothing in common with the dancing figure of Plate 54 which, by the use of powerful yet simplified rhythmic lines, suggests active and graceful movement in a manner surprisingly similar to that of modern sculpture.

The terra-cotta (literally translated from Italian as "cooked earth"—or unglazed baked clay) figurine of a woman playing either a drum or gong in Plate 55 is presented in a much more realistic and detailed way. We may learn something of Han

52. Funerary statue in gray pottery (Han).

51. Detail of a pottery tile from a tomb (Chou).

54. Pottery statuette of a dancer (Han).

costume and hair styles from this thoughtful and dignified musical figure.

All of the pictorial art of the Han dynasty survives in tombs and the offering chambers erected at their entrances. This art includes engravings on stone slabs and reliefs decorating the walls inside these chambers, pottery tiles with designs pressed into them in the underground tombs themselves, and a few painted tombs. Sometimes Chinese mythological or historical episodes were depicted, as in the pottery tile showing the meeting of two extremely important philosophers, Lao-tzŭ and Confucius (Plate 56). Confucius (551 B.C.–479 B.C.) taught the value of social duty, respect for authority, government based on moral virtues, and concern for human welfare. The followers of Lao-tzŭ, a legendary sage who was supposed to have lived during the fourth century B.C., believed in the individual rather than society, and taught that everything should be left to the wondrous workings of nature. These two philosophies deeply influenced Chinese civilization for many generations, but it was not until the Han dynasty that Confucianism became a system and Taoism—the teachings of Lao-tzŭ—a way of life.

The deeply incised tile of a stag hunt (Plate 57) also decorated a tomb. Here both horses and fleeing quarry are at a "flying gallop." Great speed and violent activity are dramatically expressed; the strong outlines have been packed with white clay so as to stand out more clearly from the typically drab background.

The pottery tiles of the third century A.D. (Plate 58) are of great importance in the history of art, as they are among the earliest painted tiles (rather than incised ones) to be discovered in China so far. They show that the artists at that time had already developed the techniques of painting to an advanced degree. The figures move and

53. Figurine of a woman carved in wood, adorned with glass and bronze (Late Chou or Early Han).

58. Painted pottery tile from tomb in Honan (Han).

55. Statuette of a female musician in painted terra-cotta (Han).

57. Gray pottery funerary tile of stag hunt (Han).

56. Pottery tile depicting the meeting of Lao-tzŭ and Confucius (Han).

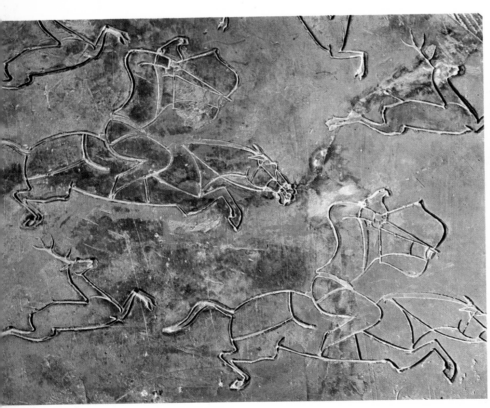

stand in easy, natural positions; and in Plate 58 the artist has tried to give a sense of perspective, or distance, by giving the two figures on the right smaller overall proportions than the other three.

Painted pottery appeared in many beautiful designs and patterns during the Han dynasty. Again, animals were frequently used as subjects.

An intricate novelty, the *po-shan-lu,* or "hill jar," appeared at this time. Only Han craftsmen were to make these interesting incense burners.

Hill jars have cone-shaped covers which have been ingeniously cast to look like hills rising up behind each other all the way to a mountainous peak; the perfumed smoke was permitted to escape from behind these "hills," which were often decorated with animals and hunting scenes. The simply decorated hill jar in Plate 59 is held up high by a laughing boy who is riding a mythological beast.

The Han dynasty also saw further refinements in the fields of jade and lacquer work. Study the delicate, intricate pattern of the silver inlay decorating the round cosmetic box made on a base of lacquer-drenched canvas in Plate 60 and the magnificent carv-

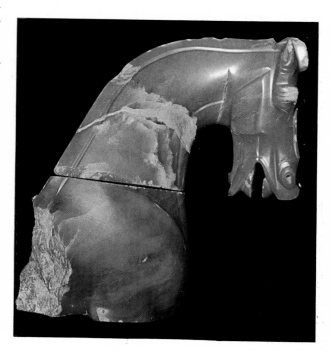

61. Head of horse in green jade (Han).

60. Lacquer box inlaid with silver (Han).

59. Hill jar with stand in form of boy and beast (Han).

ing of the three-dimensional green jade horse's head in Plate 61.

Yet it must be admitted that, on the whole, the Han period was not one of outstanding originality. Beauty was appreciated, but so was the Confucian dedication to discipline and strict social order. Therefore it is not surprising that Han art more frequently displays a refinement of past styles and decorative motifs than any striking individuality.

The great Han dynasty decayed and fell apart after four hundred years. For the next four hundred years parts of the huge Han empire were ruled by a series of Chinese and Tartar dynasties that followed one another in a confusing series, during a period called the Three Kingdoms and Six Dynasties. In the north the Wei rulers managed to unite the country for a time, but invasions by Mongols and Turks broke up China into northern and southern kingdoms in 419 A.D. Six different dynasties ruled in the north until a Tartar dynasty, the Northern Wei, again united the country for nearly a century. After that their empire was divided between the northern Ch'i and the Chou. Yet, in the end, Chinese civilization proved its enduring strength as the invading peoples gradually adopted Chinese ways.

INTRODUCTION OF BUDDHISM: The First Major Foreign Influence

Buddhism, which was to have a profound effect on Chinese life and art, was first brought to China by missionaries from India during the Han period. This religion, already four hundred years old, demanded faith from its followers and offered them through its religious doctrines a new personal hope. It is thought that the Buddha, Gautama Sākyāmuni, probably lived from 563 B.C. to 483 B.C. Buddhism broke down many of China's rigid codes of the past and led the way to individual spirituality. This could not help but have a liberating and uplifting effect on artists, for it provided them with a profound source of inspiration.

The Chinese were taught both the main schools of Buddhism—the Mahayana and the Hinayana. The Mahayana school became the most popular, and religious art flourished under its influence. Mahayana taught that salvation might be gained by prayers, contemplation, and complete devotion to a series of Buddhas ("Enlightened Ones" who had entered nirvana, a state of perfect wisdom) and bodhisattvas (who could have been Buddhas and entered nirvana but chose instead to bring salvation to mankind). Mahayana also inspired the Chinese to create religious sculpture and paintings by suggesting that such activities were a source of spiritual redemption. Hinayana's influence on art differed from that of Mahayana in that its followers preferred to represent Buddha symbolically rather than in the shape of a human form.

The noblest religious monuments left by the Northern Wei are the cave temples at Yun-kang in Shansi (fifth century A.D.) and at Lung-mên in Honan (sixth century A.D.). The earliest of such cave temples were the sanctuaries known as the Caves of the Thousand Buddhas near the oasis of Tun-huang in Kansu (see Plate 62). They were founded by the monk Lo-Tsun in 360 A.D. All these grottoes were hollowed out by hand; finishing and decorating them took many years of loving work. In Plate 63 we are shown a detail of a relief (a work of sculpture carved to stand out against a flat background surface) in marble from the cave temple of Lung-mên. It depicts, in part, a royal procession bearing religious offerings. The figures are almost life-size.

The seated statue of the Buddha Sākyāmuni, the name for the historical Buddha, is in bronze with traces of gilt (Plate 64).

We now come to three examples of Buddhist art where more than one figure is portrayed. The Buddha Sākyāmuni in Plate 65 wears the monk's robes he adopted after his "revelation." He appears with two attendants on a "votive stele," an offering to the deities set up in a temple or courtyard and usually shaped somewhat like a tombstone. "Votive stelae" (plural form) used to be commissioned from hired craftsmen by individual donors or groups of families. A modern Christian equivalent might be, roughly, giving a stained-glass window to a church. This stele, like all Buddhist sculpture in stone, clay, or wood, was originally painted; however, little of the color can be detected now on the votive stele. Plate 66 shows a complete stele, with its figures, inscriptions, and symbols carved in relief.

A splendid example of metallic Buddhist sculpture are shown in Plate 67. The gilt-

62. Cave sanctuary at Tun-huang, Kansu (fifth century A.D.).

63. Detail of relief sculpture in dark gray marble from the cave temple of Lung-mên in Honan (Northern Wei).

64. Bronze statue of seated Buddha Sākyāmuni (second half of fifth century A.D.).

bronze altarpiece presents Buddha in a blazing atmosphere of flames, flowers, animals, bodhisattvas, and heavenly beings.

Buddhism helped create religious architecture in China, and majestic and beautiful pagodas were erected in memory of Chinese rulers who had become Buddhists. Chinese pagodas, derived from earlier Nepalese temples, are architectural monuments that can have one or many stories, but never an even number. The "Pagoda of the Universe" (Plate 68) is a classic example from a later period. From a rich man's tomb, the superbly modeled pottery horse, his neck proudly arched under his ornate trappings (Plate 69), is a superior nonreligious work of the Six Dynasties.

Toward the end of the restless Six Dynasties period, the Wei empire was forcibly split into eastern and western halves. Then, in 581 A.D., Yang Chien, a minister to the northern ruler of the Ch'i, seized control and reunited all of China under his own dynasty. This dynasty was called the Sui, and it lasted a relatively short thirty-seven years. Buddhist sculpture continued to flourish as it had under the Wei. Buddhism itself had changed since the time the cave sanctuaries were cut out of the sandstone cliffs at Yun-kang in 460 A.D. At that time it was the "historical" Buddha Sākyāmuni who was most revered and most often represented in art. Then, after 500 A.D., Maitreya, Buddha of the Future, became the favorite artistic subject, retaining this prominence for fifty years. Then yet another Buddha, Amitābha, or Buddha of Boundless Splendor, captured the largest and most affectionate following. This is understandable, for spiritual rebirth for those who believed in Amitābha meant spending one's afterlife in Amitābha's Western Paradise of jeweled trees, lotus ponds, breathtaking palaces, celestial music, and dancing. The large

bronze altarpiece in Plate 70 shows Amitābha seated on a jeweled lotus throne in the exotic atmosphere of his Western Paradise. Four smaller figures on either side of him are partly concealed by the two bodhisattvas —Avalokitésvara on the right, holding a pomegranate, and Mahastamaprapta on the left, his hands clasped in prayer. These two represent compassion and wisdom.

Under the influence of "Paradise cults," the arts became less coldly distant and dignified. Figures became more human, ornaments more elaborate, drapery more natural. These differences can be observed by comparing certain features of the two striking

65. Votive stele representing Buddha Sākyāmuni, in high relief against green leaf-shaped screen (Six Dynasties, sixth century A.D.).

66. Buddhist stele in terra-cotta (Northern Wei, sixth century A.D.).

67. Altarpiece in gilt bronze (524 A.D.).

68. Pagoda of the Universe at Hangchow.

69. Pottery horse (Northern Wei, c. 530 A.D.).

Sui bodhisattvas in Plates 71 and 72. Both wear ornate robes and are adorned with ropes of pearls and other regal jewelry. Yet one poses with the severe authority of a column and is nobly expressionless, while the other bodhisattva, Avalokitésvara, radiates smiling charm as he relaxes gracefully with his weight on his left leg and his right knee thrust forward like a dancer at ease. His rounded face and hands as well as his luxurious costume show a direct influence from Indian art.

History seemed to repeat itself once more; extravagance, corruption, and dark plots within the court brought about the downfall of the Sui dynasty. In the confusion, a young soldier named Li Shih-min, who had successfully started revolutionary movements when still only sixteen years old, triumphed and made himself T'ang emperor in 618 A.D.

71. Statue of bodhisattva (Sui).

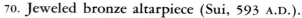

72. Statue of bodhisattva Avalokitésvara in stone (Sui, late sixth century A.D.).

70. Jeweled bronze altarpiece (Sui, 593 A.D.).

THE T'ANG DYNASTY
China's Most Brilliant Period

The T'ang dynasty was in power for three hundred years, and this period was to prove the most brilliant period in all of China's history. Old territories were recaptured, and the empire was extended to Vietnam and Korea, to the remote region of Tibet, stretching from Annam (in modern Vietnam) to distant Turkistan. Foreign trade thrived as never before, bringing political and cultural contacts with many different countries and areas, including the Middle East. Buddhist priests from India, officials and merchants from Persia and the central Asian kingdoms, Arabs, Turks, and Nestorian Christians came and often settled in China, and built mosques, temples, and churches. The T'ang capital of Ch'ang-an, about the size of modern Paris, became the greatest and most cosmopolitan city in the world. All these foreign influences enriched the arts by introducing new styles and motifs; and Chinese civilization was strong enough to absorb them without losing its own individual character. This period has also been called the Golden Age of Poetry; suddenly poets and painters were being entertained by emperors and their relatives in palaces and great houses.

The opulence and elegance of the T'ang dynasty can be summed up by the Buddha shown in Plate 73. We must try to imagine him in his original coats of brilliant paint. His missing hands were evidently lying one on top of the other in the gesture of meditation. Buddhist cave temples were enhanced by enormous naturalistic figures of awesome proportions, such as those in the temple dedicated to Buddha Vairocana, who was at the center of the spiritual world. The temple was at Lung-mên in Honan (Plate 74). (The scale of the great images is indicated by the group of people in the entrance of the temple.)

Two remarkably different interpretations of the bodhisattva Avalokitésvara, Lord of Compassion, can be compared in Plates 75 and 76. The Chinese gradually changed not only his name but his sex as well, and later he emerged as Kuan-yin, the adored Goddess of Mercy. The stone statue (Plate 75) owes its softly realistic physical style again to India; the carved ivory figure (Plate 76), holding its emblem—a basket of fish—appears more typically Chinese.

A truly imposing T'ang creation is the magnificent bronze sarcophagus (a glorified coffin) seen in Plate 77. It is embellished with a dragon and supported by the four

73. **Figure of Buddha in painted stone (T'ang).**

74. Temple dedicated to the Buddha Vairocana, Lung-mên, Honan (T'ang).

75. Stone statue of the bodhisattva Avalokitésvara, or Kuan-yin (T'ang, eighth century).

76. Ivory statuette of Kuan-yin, Chinese version of the bodhisattva Avalokitésvara (probably T'ang).

guardians of the four quarters, or directions, who traditionally guarded the world and the Buddhist faith. They were known as lokapalas and appear most usually in fiercely protective postures. The fearsome lokapala in Plate 78 was carved and painted to look like a soldier of the victorious T'ang armies, and his raised arm evidently held a weapon. The more terrible their expression, the more effective were their powers against evil spirits—so thought the Chinese.

With the powerful T'ang dynasty, exceptionally fine ceramics were produced on a very large scale, mostly to be exported. The

T'ang ceramics were sought after for both their artistry and their superb decorative qualities. They are often covered with glassy lead enamel glazes of various extremely deep colors (mostly orange, spinach green, and lemon yellow, more rarely blue), which were sometimes permitted to trickle freely from the top to the bottom of a piece of pottery, thereby creating a bright and showy polychromatic (multicolored) decoration.

For examples of the use of these color combinations, see Plates 79, 80. The lion biting his paw illustrates the trickling glaze technique. The brown jar with small loop handles and a flattened shape in Plate 80 is a most interesting object—a "pilgrim flask." Many Chinese Buddhists made long pil-grimages across central Asia to visit the holy places of Buddhism in India, and they used these flasks for water, wines, and other liquids.

During the T'ang dynasty, ceramic figures of caravan camels (see Plate 81) began to be buried in tombs, giving evidence of that period's progress in trade and travel. Here again we see trickled glaze used to achieve a most successful—and colorful—effect.

T'ang emperors and courtiers cared passionately for horses; some kept stables of thousands upon thousands. Polo, a most popular royal sport, was brought from Persia in the reign of the first T'ang emperor and was shortly taken up as subject matter by craftsmen. The figures of horses are the greatest triumphs of T'ang potters. Stand-

77. **Bronze sarcophagus supported by four guardians (T'ang, eighth century).**

78. Carved lokapala in painted wood from Tun-huang (T'ang).

ing, prancing, or galloping, these splendid creatures live again in their tomb models. A statuette in unglazed pottery shows a lady playing polo (Plate 82). Several such horsewomen have been found among T'ang grave figures, and poems by the great Li Po or his imitators describe the rides in the parks of Ch'ang-an by Yang Kuei-fei, the favorite of Emperor Ming-huang, and by other beauties of the T'ang court.

Charming dancing girls with long snake-like sleeves that cover their hands were also immortalized, in painted pale-pink clay (Plate 83).

With the pictures *Tuning the Lute and Drinking Tea* (Plate 84), *The Journey of the Emperor Ming-huang to Shu* (Plate 85) and, *Portrait of Fu Shêng* (Plate 86), we enter a rapidly advancing phase of Chinese painting. The names of several great T'ang painters have been preserved, though their works have long since disappeared; luckily, however, copies made from the originals in the tenth and eleventh centuries give some idea of their greatness. This applies to the hand scroll *Tuning the Lute and Drinking Tea* (Plate 84), which was copied two to three hundred years after the original was completed. At first glance this seems to be a very simple painting, but closer examina-

79. Glazed pottery lion (T'ang).

80. "Pilgrim flask" type of bottle in glazed earthenware (T'ang).

82. Statuette of lady playing polo, in unglazed pottery (T'ang).

81. Glazed pottery camel (T'ang).

tion reveals the great care with which the artist has placed his figures and varied their scale to give a sense of space. Also notice, for example, how the red shape, which is simply a flat area of color, seems to contain a leaning, living, three-dimensional

84. *Tuning the Lute and Drinking Tea,* hand scroll, ink and watercolor on paper, attributed to Chou Fang (T'ang).

83. Figurine of dancing girl, in unglazed pottery (T'ang).

85. *The Journey of the Emperor Ming-huang to Shu,* hanging scroll, ink and watercolor on silk (T'ang).

86. *Portrait of Fu Shêng,* hand scroll, ink and watercolor on silk (T'ang).

human being, while a flat rock and two slender trees give the calm and ordered feeling of a carefully cultivated palace garden in a timeless world. T'ang pictures cover the three basic types and shapes that were to become traditional in China: the vertically hung wall scroll (Plate 85), the album leaf, and the horizontal hand scroll (Plates 84, 86). The last category is particularly interesting in that the artist's work was not viewed all at once; instead the viewer was meant to unroll the painted scroll little by little, slowly and patiently, and thus to enjoy fully the flowing changes of scene being depicted. *Potrait of Fu Shêng,* itself a hand scroll of this type, shows the painter unrolling a hand scroll before spreading it out to work on it. During the T'ang period, a fairly wide variety of subjects and types were used by painters: scenes of court life, scenes based on historical anecdotes, paintings of horses, portraits of famous persons and literary and mythological characters. At that time artists started painting landscapes, which, because of their dominant colors, have come to be called "blue-green."

With the downfall of the T'ang and the coming of the Sung dynasty, landscape became the chief theme and enjoyed a golden age, assuming, not only in Chinese painting but in Oriental painting in general, a position of importance as one of the world's great classic arts, still admired today.

Fifty years of trouble and strife followed the end of the T'ang dynasty. This is called the "Five Dynasties" period. Many conquered territories either broke away from China or were captured by Arabs in the west or Mongols in the north. There were other signs of disintegration: Usurpers and minor princes snatched for themselves whatever areas they could; international trade slowly died; and Confucians launched an inhuman persecution of the Buddhists. Thousands of monasteries and religious buildings were destroyed. Nevertheless, the Five Dynasties era was, rather unexpectedly, an exciting and productive time for Chinese painting. Academies of art were founded, and collectors became active. Painting was sponsored in various provincial courts, such as those of Nanking and Chengtu.

Landscape painting (in Chinese, *shanshin,* meaning "mountains and water") began to interest the majority of artists during the tenth century. *Deer in Autumn Landscape* (Plate 87), a hanging scroll in ink and watercolor on silk, is a marvelous example of Five Dynasties art at its observant best. This beautiful composition shows a stag and seven does in a clearing beside a stream among autumn leaves. The feathery leaves are painted with complete accuracy, and the different colors are massed together to form an overall pattern suggesting a tapestry. The type of vast landscape that is always painted as if seen from a height came into fashion at this time; and there was another artistic innovation as the

painters of the Five Dynasties period, using washes of India ink, created what is called a monochrome, or one-colored, landscape. Chinese painting is done in black ink and

87. *Deer in Autumn Landscape,* hanging scroll, ink and watercolor on silk (Five Dynasties).

watercolor, or in ink alone, on silk or paper. The dry ink is made of pine or oil soot mixed with glue; it is then ground on a flat stone and mixed with a little water before the brush is dipped into it. Its density, or darkness, depends on how much water is added; the more diluted the ink, the lighter the shade. The brush is of the type we use for watercolors today and has a fine, pointed tip. With the side of a brush heavily loaded with ink or color, large, even areas—such as sky—can be "washed in." Holding the brush in other positions can produce thick or thin lines, firm or wavering ones. "Drybrush" means a way of using the least water possible when picking up the ink; this way there is no chance at all of "running," and the brush can be used like a broad black crayon or, using the tip alone, like a finely sharpened drawing pencil.

THE SUNG DYNASTY:
The Golden Age of Landscape Painting

In 960 A.D. the last independent state of those once ruled by the Five Dynasties submitted to Sung rule (960–1279 A.D.), which was subsequently divided into two periods. The first period, during which the Sung emperors ruled all China except Kansu and the region around Peking, lasted from 960 to 1127 A.D. The second period started in 1128, with Tartars occupying the north and the Sung reigning only part of their original empire in southern China. This period we term the Southern Sung. The early period is often called the Northern Sung dynasty. The Southern Sung emperors made Hangchow their capital. This period ended with total Mongol conquest in 1279. Even when their territories included nearly all of China, the Sung never had the same contacts and commerce with, or interest in, the outside world as the T'ang. The centuries-long Moslem conquests in India and the gradual disappearance of Buddhism there cut all ties between Chinese and Indian Buddhists. China, which had been the center of the civilized world under the T'ang, went back to her own traditions and became a world in herself, apart.

88. *Listening to the Wind in the Pines,* hanging scroll, ink and watercolor on silk, by Ma Lin (dated 1246).

89. *Walking along a Mountain Path in Spring,* album painting, ink and light color on silk, by Ma Yüan (Sung).

Despite constant threats from Tartars on the northern borders as well as internal rivalries, the period of Sung rule was a brilliant epoch for the arts. The Sung emperors, almost without exception, were generous patrons of scholarship and painting, and one of them commissioned a thousand-volume encyclopedia. Scholars, philosophers, and respected sages became an inspiration for painters, appearing in such pictures as *Listening to the Wind in the Pines* (Plate 88), and *Walking along a Mountain Path in Spring* (Plate 89). In the first, the scholar, framed by meticulously painted boughs and roots of a willow, has abandoned himself to deep reflection and seems almost to be at one with nature.

Never has a civilization taken greater spiritual interest in nature than did that of the Chinese; in fact the expression "com-

muning with nature" could be said to be the artistic foundation of much of Chinese art, particularly landscape painting. Their sense of "universality" and harmony in all areas of spiritual and physical life has been a constant source of philosophical inspiration for the Chinese. Its preoccupying effects on artists have produced works of sensitive genius. This is borne out by the scroll by Ma Lin (Plate 88) in which a scholar, tense and alert, is absorbed by the wind in the pines. The expression of rapt concentration on his face is not that of a person who is simply listening for storm warnings or any other such practicality; it is the expression of one who hears something almost supernatural, a message or a strain of music that only a person of his refinement and sensitivity could perceive. The miniature man in the lower left corner

90. *Waiting for Friends by the Light of Lanterns,* album painting, ink and watercolor on silk, by Ma Lin (Sung).

is intended to be a boy, a young scholar attending his master devotedly. A similar boy apprentice follows a sage into a seemingly infinite expanse of springtime and distance in Plate 89. This haunting effect is achieved by having almost every line and shape move from the lower left corner toward the upper right corner, which is left deliberately bare of any line or wash. The painter, Ma Yüan, was a celebrated master and earned the nickname "One-corner Ma" for his characteristic style. The name is taken from a saying of Confucius which ends ". . . I show one corner, and if a man cannot find the other three, I am not going to repeat myself."

Waiting for Friends by the Light of Lanterns makes us read our own story of anticipation or loneliness into it (Plate 90).

We come to examples of paintings (Plates 91, 92) which show the magnificent Sung landscapes at their most sweeping. This sort of landscape is the supreme achievement of the Sung artists and was to dominate Chinese painting in later generations. A painting academy was started at K'ai fēng by Emperor Hui-tsung (1101–1126 A.D.), who was himself a talented painter (see Plate 91) as well as a passionate collector of archaic bronzes and jade carvings. At the beginning of his reign he laid down a rule for the academy: "Painters are not to imitate their predecessors, but are to depict objects as they exist, true to color and form." The Taoist view of painting, which was important to leading artists, went further than this, for it maintained that if an artist was to succeed, whoever looked at his picture must react to it as he would to the actual objects themselves, just as the artist had originally. The standard words of praise for a landscape in Sung critical literature are that "it makes one feel as if one were really in the place depicted."

In the Sung dynasty of the eleventh century, however, a different view of painting was taken by scholars and art lovers. They now held that how an artist *felt* about his subject was more important than how accurately he reproduced that subject in his paintings. In other words, the mind of the painter became the real subject of the painting. If the picture was to mirror the man, it therefore followed that the best paintings would be done by men of learning, refinement, and good character, such as the Confucian scholars aimed at being. This school of "literati" (literate ones) painting, taken up by scholars who painted in their leisure time, eventually became a strong influence in Chinese painting and overshadowed the artistic traditions developed by generations of professional painters.

The Ch'an Buddhist school grew up in the monasteries around Hangchow, the Sung capital, and used a "rough brush" technique that was also adopted by the amateur literati. Suddenness and spontaneity of the rough brush characterize Ch'an methods of painting. Feeling had to be expressed to the viewer in a direct, immediate impression of the subject painted.

91. *Autumn in the Hills and River Valley,* hanging scroll, attributed to Emperor Hui-tsung (Sung).

92. *Landscape in Wind and Rain,* hanging scroll, watercolor on silk, attributed to Ma Yüan (Sung).

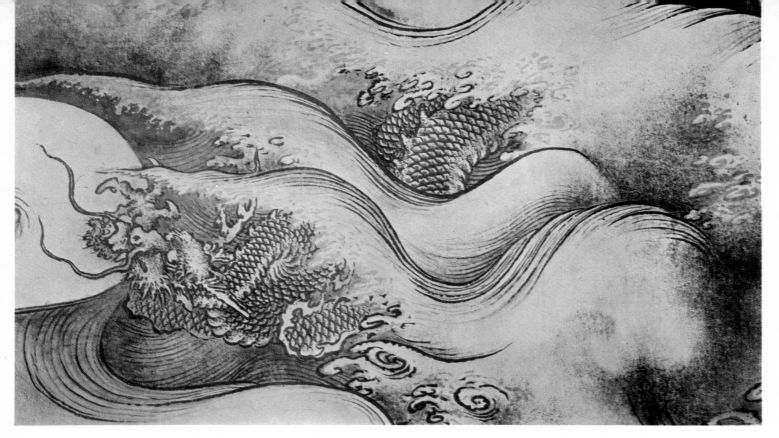

93. *The Nine Dragons* (detail), ink and watercolor on paper, by Ch'en Jung (Sung).

94. *Tribute Bearers on Horseback,* hanging scroll, ink and watercolor on silk (twelfth century).

95. *The Han Palaces,* album painting, ink and watercolor on silk, attributed to Chao Po-chu (twelfth century).

46

Sung painting was by no means confined to majestic landscapes. Wildly imaginative decorations appeared, such as the fearsome dragon in a boiling sea that made up part of a large screen called *The Nine Dragons* (Plate 93). The past was being recalled in such works as the hanging scroll entitled *Tribute Bearers on Horseback* (Plate 94); with its delicate colors against a somber background and its Persian, fairy-tale air, this work was most probably copied from a scroll of the T'ang dynasty, when tribute was periodically sent to the emperors from Asia and the Middle East.

Rather than simply imitating an earlier period, the album picture *The Han Palaces* (Plate 95) is imaginary, an artist's dreamlike vision of the legendary palaces of the Han. The album painting *The Traveling Peddler* (Plate 96), on the other hand, was drawn from everyday life and therefore is considered a "genre" painting. "Genre" painting means that a picture shows some aspect of daily life. This village scene is painted with humanity and humor; one wonders what hilarious catastrophe is going to happen thanks to the child whose curiosity as to the peddler's wares cannot be contained.

Portraits, too, could sometimes be imaginary, as in the case of *The Poet Li Po* (Plate 97); Li Po, though long-dead, was nevertheless portrayed by Liang-K'ai—in the rough-brush, or "untrammeled," style—gazing at the moon and chanting a poem. Other portraits, including *Portrait of the Ch'an Master Wu-Chün* (Plate 98), were taken from life. This particular hanging scroll has great strength of both composition and color,

96. *The Traveling Peddler,* album painting, ink and light color on silk, signed by Li Sung (1210).

97. *The Poet Li Po,* hanging scroll, ink on paper, by Liang K'ai (mid-thirteenth century).

which nonetheless emphasizes the sensitivity of the subject's expression rather than detracting from it.

Birds and flowers were painted with fine brushwork, elegance, and loving observation in the Sung period, and certain combinations of them came to be traditional—bamboo trees and sparrows, lotus flowers and water

99. *Sparrows Perching on Bamboo,* hanging scroll, ink and watercolor on paper, attributed to Mu-ch'i (mid-thirteenth century).

98. *Portrait of the Ch'an Master Wu-Chün,* hanging scroll, ink and watercolor on silk (1238).

101. *Birds and Plum Blossom,* painting, attributed to Ma Lin (thirteenth century).

102. *The Hundred Wild Geese,* section of a hand scroll, ink and color on paper, attributed to Ma Fên (twelfth century).

100. *Quail,* album leaf, color on silk, attributed to Li An-chung (twelfth century).

birds, willows and swallows, peonies and peacocks, etc. *Sparrows Perching on Bamboo* (Plate 99) is a perfect little painting that illustrates what the artist could achieve with a minimum of strokes. *Quail* (Plate 100)

is believed to have been painted by Li An-chung (1120–1160), an artist of the Southern Sung Academy known for his delicate pictures of this particular bird. Notice how minutely the feathers are painted in light and dark colors; the artist has left the surface bare, with only the background color used for the middle tones. *Birds and Plum Blossom* (Plate 101) has been attributed to Ma Lin. This artist, the son of "One-corner Ma," came from a family of painters who worked at the Imperial Academy for five generations. Ma Lin, whom we have met before, painted landscapes (Plates 88, 90) and birds with flowers competently and with great charm. In this example, the outlines of the branches are heavily drawn, in contrast to the softness of the birds' plumage.

We are shown only six of *The Hundred Wild Geese* in Plate 102, a section of a hand scroll. Nevertheless even that is quite enough for us to be amazed by the artist's ability to combine artistic freedom with long

103. *Lotus Flowers and Water Bird,* hanging scroll, color on silk, by Te Ch'ien (Sung).

Sculpture in the early, or Northern, Sung period continued more or less in the T'ang tradition. But after the Tartar conquests of the eleventh and twelfth centuries Buddhism regained some of its vitality and inspiration. Figures of lohans, some of which may be actual portraits, appeared, made of pottery or dried lacquer, this last being a most interesting technique. Lohans were deeply devout men, half-hermit, half-saint, who could be either monks or meditative recluses. The glazed pottery lohan in Plate 104 is slightly over life-size, extremely formal, and yet imposingly alive with his burning, trancelike expression of heavenly meditation. Both the seated lohan and the authoritative lohan head in Plates 105 and 106 are executed in dry lacquer. To begin this process, a clay model would be made; next, cloth soaked in lacquer would be smoothed over the clay and left to dry. Sometimes a coating of fine plaster would then be spread over the lacquered cloth so that fine details could be picked out in it. Finally the clay would be scraped and chipped from the core, and the resulting work of art would be hollow and light yet very durable. All that was left to do was to paint it.

Bodhisattvas had not lost their popularity as subjects in the second Sung period (see Plate 107), particularly the eternally beloved and sex-changed Kuan-yin, Goddess of Mercy. In a fragment of a wall painting (Plate 108) she is seen in all her detailed finery, holding a rain vase or ambrosia bottle. In sculpture she is represented as a tranquil, protective figure wearing long, elaborate robes, necklaces, and a tiara—dignified yet more human than ever before (Plates 109, 110). She is usually seated in the position of "royal ease," with one leg raised and the knee supporting her outstretched arm. The soft, rounded modeling

and patient zoological study. The beautiful *Lotus Flowers and Water Bird* (Plate 103) is just one of many such hanging scrolls that were created by a special school of flower painting which flourished during the Sung period in the fertile countryside south of the Yangtse River. This school was later carried on by the families of professional painters, who handed down their techniques from father to son through the generations.

105. Seated lohan, in dried lacquer (1099).

107. Statue of bodhisattva in wood with traces of paint (Liao or Ch'in, during time of Sung dynasty).

104. Glazed pottery lohan (Sung).

108. Fragment of a fresco showing bodhisattva Kuan-yin (twelfth century).

106. Head of a lohan, in dried lacquer (tenth to twelfth centuries).

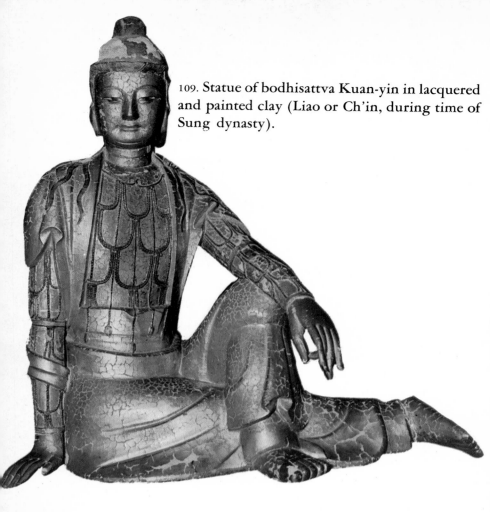

109. Statue of bodhisattva Kuan-yin in lacquered and painted clay (Liao or Ch'in, during time of Sung dynasty).

110. Bodhisattva Avalokitésvara or Kuan-yin (twelfth century).

111. Jade vessel in the form of a bronze *kuei* (Sung, thirteenth to fourteenth centuries).

of face, hands, and body creates the impression of a living being, and the gentle sweetness of these Kuan-yin images is beautiful and moving.

As mentioned earlier, the Sung emperors and the members of their courts became passionate antique collectors and they loved objects that took their designs from ancient times. The jade vessel in Plate 111 is in the form of an ancient bronze *kuei* with an ancient motif, dragon heads on the handles. The beautifully carved jade ornament in Plate 112 also was inspired by antique forms and dragon heads.

Archaic designs were adapted to one of China's most famous artistic achievements—porcelain. The first type of porcelain to be produced is known as "proto porcelain," and it appeared as early as the Six Dynasties period (265–589 A.D.); an example of it, a ceramic halfway between the glazed ceramics of the Han dynasty and true porcelain of the T'ang dynasty, is the animal-shaped vessel in Plate 113. T'ang porcelains frequently imitated foreign forms, as, for instance, the white vase in Plate 114, which is in shape of a Greek amphora (a vessel usually used for oil or wine) and has a stopper representing a phoenix, the legendary bird that rises from its own ashes. The *huai* kettle is northern celadon stoneware, a gray or tan ware with a transparent brown or gray glaze. The style of its carved decoration is related to that used in *Ting* ware (see Plate 115). *Ting* ware is true porcelain. True porcelain is made basically from kaolin, a fine white clay, and sometimes has glazes made from the mineral feldspar. The English word "kaolin" comes from the Chinese *Kao-ling,* meaning "high hill"; this was the name of

113. **Animal-shaped vessel in proto porcelain** (Six Dynasties).

114. **Greek-influenced white porcelain vase** (T'ang).

112. **Green jade plaque (Sung).**

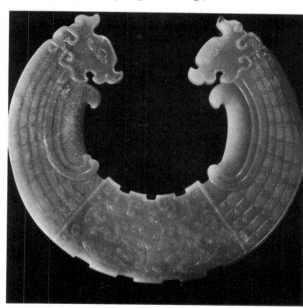

115. *Ting* **bowl, white porcelain with transparent glaze (Sung).**

116. Glazed ceramic vase of *Tz'ŭ-chou* type (Sung).

a mountain from which kaolin was first taken to be exported to Europe.

The many-colored, lead-glazed pottery so common in the T'ang period is no longer found in the Sung period. Some of the best-known and most perfect types of Sung ceramics are the *Tz'ŭ-chou* painted ware, fine in both design and technique (Plates 116, 117); *Ting*, the white porcelain with transparent ivory or cream glaze; the different types of celadon; *Chien*, a heavy stoneware which was famous and much used in Japan (Plate 118); and *Chün* ware, in simple shapes and bright colors (Plates 119, 120, 121).

Early in the thirteenth century the Mongol tribes of the northern steppes were welded into a huge and terrifying army by Genghis Khan, one of history's greatest conquerors. His ruthless horsemen swept

118. *Chien* ware jar (Sung).

117. Glazed ceramic "bottle vase" (Sung).

119. *Chün* cup with light blue glaze (Sung).

120. *Chün* ceramic jar with blue and purple glaze (Sung).

121. *Chün* flowerpot vase with mottled blue and red glaze (Sung).

across central Asia to the Caspian Sea and beyond, and across the Great Wall into China. The Chin Tartars in north China were overwhelmed (they had become as refined as the civilization they had overrun), and the last Sung defenses were broken down by the 1270's.

THE YÜAN DYNASTY:
Time of the Mongols

Kublai Khan, the grandson of Genghis Khan, had transferred his capital from Karakorum in Mongolia to Peking, and here he was proclaimed emperor of China in 1260 though his final defeat of the Sung did not come until 1279. (Peking had been captured by his grandfather in 1215). In other countries he was looked upon as a ruthless conqueror. However, this did not prevent countries outside of China from sending emissaries, craftsmen, and merchants to the magnificent court of the great Kublai, and among the visiting foreigners was Marco Polo of Venice. The first European reports on China appeared at this time, written by travelers who had made the journey across central Asia (for the Mongols, who could be very destructive, at least kept their roads in good enough condition for safe and relatively fast travel). Marco Polo was amazed by the splendor of Chinese cities, particularly Hangchow. Hangchow had kept up the rhythm of leisure and luxury that had been fostered by the Southern Sung when they made the city their capital. Dennis Bloodworth, author of *The Chinese Looking Glass,* describes the city as a place of "pleasure gardens and pagodas, of leisurely excursions in painted lake barges, of taverns in which rice wine was served in silver cups and restaurants that specialized in this or that delicacy, including the ices that Marco Polo later introduced to Italy. . . . There was a brisk business in antiques for wealthy connoisseurs, and dozens of shops sold merchandise unheard of in the West—ingenious toys, printed books, painted fans, anti-mosquito powder, drugs out of the capacious Chinese pharmacopoeia."

Kublai Khan was an intelligent man, an enlightened ruler who respected and admired Chinese culture. He even took the Chinese name "Yüan" for his dynasty, which was to last about a century. He brought China back to a state of prosperity after years of war and strife by encouraging agriculture and foreign trade and by constructing canals and highways. He made Peking one of the most beautiful cities in China.

The Mongol court at the new capital never became the all-powerful center of Chinese cultural life that the Sung or T'ang courts had been, in spite of Kublai Khan's encouragement of scholars and artists. Many Confucian scholars refused to serve a foreign ruler and went into retirement. Some took to the experimental writing of novels and plays as a creative form, while others with a talent for painting worked only for their own enjoyment and that of intimate friends.

The Imperial Academy was dead, and suddenly the traditional styles of painting seemed old-fashioned and stale to young would-be artists. Nevertheless, the rebirth of the amateur "literati" school of painting provided one important development in the history of Yüan art. The followers of this school were cast in the same mold as their forebears, whom we mentioned earlier. They were scholars and gentlemen who often also wrote poetry in the fine calligraphy that was the proof of a complete education. It is typical of their intellectual approach to most matters that they preferred to concentrate on the technical problems posed by a painting rather than to attempt fresh and imaginative subjects and themes.

They looked neither to the present nor to the future, but turned back to the masters of landscape of the tenth and eleventh centuries, who had painted full, detailed compositions. They abandoned the beautifully mysterious and mistily romantic empty spaces that late Southern Sung painters like Ma Yüan and Hsia Kuei had so hauntingly developed and instead crowded their scrolls with highly detailed rocks and foliage, limbs and mountains, miniature houses, tiny boats, and, on some occasions, figures so minuscule as to be nearly invisible.

Artists became more and more preoccupied with the effects of individual brush-strokes either alone or in carefully studied combinations. Painting and calligraphy drew closer together than ever before. This marriage of arts found its ultimate expression with the perfection of a special branch of Chinese art—bamboo painting. In this art the bamboo became the favorite theme. To explain all the reasons why such a seemingly limited form of artistic expression was admired to the point of reverence would take far too long; but we can, at least, thoughtfully consider several of the basic Chinese attitudes that brought about this unique artistic development. The first is their respect for the bamboo plant as a symbol for the Confucian "superior man," who, like the plant, would bend with prevailing winds but not break. In other words, the ideal man adapted himself to life as demanded by society but did not permit his spirit or integrity to be snapped by it. Then, too, the written word, particularly in poetry, and the art of painting have always been held in higher esteem by the Chinese than even the finest in sculpture, ceramic design, or musical composition. This may seem illogical to Western ways of thinking, but the reason lies again in the high regard of the Chinese for personal expression and in their deep spiritual interest in nature. Calligraphy, or the art of handwriting, was originally a development of a series of symbolic figures known today as pictograms; these, fittingly enough, were basically inspired by nature. Individual writing techniques, or the visual manner in which these pictograms were drawn with brush and ink, were as deeply appreciated by serious art lovers as were the traditional scrolls of endless gorges, craggy peaks, nodding chrysanthemums, or darting sparrows. Bamboo painting is closer to calligraphy than any other art form and is so extremely stylized that a special flexible, pointed brush is used so that each leaf may spring to life with one deft stroke. Writing appears prominently in bamboo paintings, as in *Bamboo* (Plate 122), a detail from an album by Wu Chên (1280–1354), a poet and calligrapher who became a Taoist hermit, and in the strong, graceful *Bamboo and Chrysanthemums* (Plate 123), a hanging scroll signed by K'o Chiu-ssu (1290–1343).

The chief figure in the Yüan revival of painting was Chao Mêng-fu (1254–1322), an exceptionally gifted man and the greatest

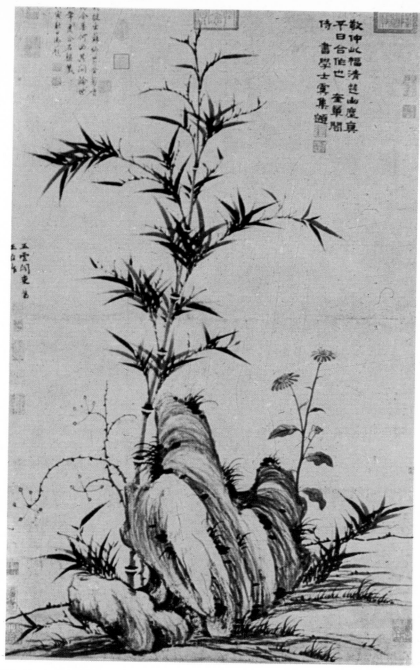

123. *Bamboo and Chrysanthemums,* hanging scroll, ink on paper, signed by K'o Chiu-ssu (Yüan, 1290–1343).

122. *Bamboo* (detail), from an album by Wu Chên (Yüan, 1280–1354).

calligrapher of his day. He was a government official who rose to a position of great importance, and was also a Confucian scholar who has studied Buddhism and Taoism. He had served under the Sung, but unlike many of the Confucians, he accepted Kublai Khan's invitation to join his court. He painted landscapes, figures, and flowers, but, not surprisingly, it was his pictures of horses which most appealed to the roughriding Mongols. His *Autumn Colors in the Ch'iao and Hua Mountains* (Plate 124), from a hand scroll, is painted in ink and light colors on paper. There is nothing new about the subject matter when compared with that of paintings of the past, but in this case Chao Mêng-fu, who had studied the old masters of landscape, gave it his own entirely new and delicately colored interpretation. Various types of fine strokes can be noticed, from the featheriness of the leaves and lake plants to the firm outlines of the tree trunks and the heavy shading of the distant mountaintop.

Shêng Mou also painted landscapes in a highly individual, descriptive style. In his *Boating on the River in Autumn* (Plate 125), we are shown a breathtaking variety of techniques. The trees have been "splashed in," loose color areas are controlled by hard

124. *Autumn Colors in the Ch'iao and Hua Mountains,* from a hand scroll, ink and light colors on paper, signed by Chao Mêng-fu (Yüan, 1254–1322).

125. *Boating on the River in Autumn,* hand scroll, signed by Shêng Mou (Yüan).

126. *Dwellings in the Hills in Autumn,* hanging scroll, ink and colors on paper, signed by Wang Mêng (Yüan).

and soft lines and countless small dots, and the fishermen have been painstakingly rendered in "drybrush," in this instance the brush having been used like a sharpened hard pastel stick.

Four of the best landscape painters working in the first half of the fourteenth century were Huang Kung-wang, Wang Mêng, Wu Chên, whom we have already mentioned, and Ni Tsan. Each painted in a distinctive style that influenced later artists. Paintings by Huang Kung-wang are extremely rare; it is said that he retired from the world to live and paint in the mountains. Wang Mêng's scrolls are often tall and narrow, with masses of rocks and mountains surging from the base and receding into the distance in an almost forbidding manner. In his *Dwellings in the Hills in Autumn* (Plate 126), the eye is led from a peaceful little fishing scene in the foreground through miraculously detailed trees to a harsh and frightening summit, the whole composition seeming to suggest, as do so many Chinese landscapes, the relentless power of raw nature in contrast to the fleeting existence of mere man.

Ni Tsan was a wealthy man of leisure who gave away his beautiful house with its garden, library, and art collection to live with his wife on a houseboat. He wandered up and down the streams and lakes of Kiangsu, painting the scenery. He used a limited range of light silvery tones in very dry ink, and his compositions are simple and austere. They consist of plain, uncomplicated settings, as in *Mountain Scenery with a Little House on the River* (Plate 127), with no rising mists, only such straightforward aspects of nature as a few slender trees springing from rocky ground, expanses of lake, and bare hills in the distance. The differences between his works and a "literati" painting such as *The Patriarch Pu-tai* (Plate 128), a hand scroll by Yin T'o-lo, are obvious at first glance. In this last picture, the artist has worked very quickly in shades of the same color ink; the lines and shapes quickly

127. *Mountain Scenery with a Little House on the River,* hanging scroll, ink on paper, signed by Ni Tsan (Yüan).

128. *The Patriarch Pu-tai,* hand scroll, ink on paper, signed by Yin T'o-lo (Yüan).

129. *Seated Lohan,* hanging scroll, colors on silk, attributed to anonymous Buddhist painter (Yüan).

130. *Landscape,* hanging scroll, ink and colors on silk, signed by Sun Chün-tsê (Yüan).

sum up a scene with spontaneity and freedom. The term "expressionism" is used to describe this effective style, not to be confused with the European and American style of painting also known as "Expressionism."

As in most periods of art, there are the exceptions to the current rule, and we come across such exceptions in *Seated Lohan* (Plate 129), a hanging scroll in colors on silk, and

Landscape (Plate 130), a hanging scroll signed by Sun Chün-tsê. The lohan is evidently by a Buddhist painter who has imitated the style of a T'ang monk and artist named Kuan-hsiu, while the landscape, with its background fading into empty space and its melancholy little pavilion, could easily be mistaken for an authentic painting of the Southern Sung period.

Individual statues of great beauty and merit were still being created in the four-teenth century in the rich and realistic manner of late Sung Buddhist sculpture. The painted wooden figures of Kuan-yin, Goddess of Mercy, in Plates 131 and 132 have been carved with great skill and atten-tion to detail, but they are somewhat out-shone by the brilliantly gilded and painted masterpiece of grace and elegance seen in Plate 133. This Kuan-yin, who sits poised on a rock with her feet resting on a lotus plant, is an unqualified triumph of the early Yüan period.

The Mongols loved the sumptuous glitter

131.

Two statues of Kuan-yin in painted wood (Yüan).

132.

133. Statue of Kuan-yin in painted and gilded wood (Yüan).

134. Rosette-shaped silver plate (Yüan).

135. Blue-and-white pottery vase (Yüan).

of silver and gold. Chinese craftsmen were kept hard at work supplying their demands for elaborate utensils, such as the rosette-shaped silver dish shown in Plate 134, which closely follows the lines of some of the T'ang bronze mirrors. Yüan potters tried to follow the styles set during the Sung dynasty, but while the shapes of their wares were frequently pleasing, their colors, nonetheless, did not have the brilliance of the great Chinese periods (see Plate 135). A ceramic object of unusual interest can be

136. Headrest in *chün* ware (Yüan).

seen in Plate 136. This which is a headrest is glazed much like *Sung chün* ware (see Plates 119, 120, 121).

After Kublai Khan there were no Mongol emperors of any ability. The country became disastrously poor owing to the government's inability to handle economic matters. Ultimately, the peasants would stand for no more. Revolts took place in southern China, organized by secret societies such as the White Lotus, and a few years later a more serious rebellion was led by Chu Yüan-chang, a monk turned politician. The Chinese never had acknowledged the Mongols as anything better than barbaric foreigners who, to add insult to injury, had insisted on treating them as inferior citizens in their own country. Chu Yüan-chang was himself born a peasant. His mother and father died of the plague while he was still a young boy, and it was only through the charitable efforts of a monastery that he was able to survive.

Monks frequently were obliged to travel alone along lonely, dangerous roads and consequently fell natural prey to bandits.

The earliest known forms of judo were developed as a means of monastic self-preservation, and openhanded karate was also practiced for chopping firewood in monastery kitchens, where no axes were permitted. Thus, Chu Yüan-chang was exposed, in the monastery, to a toughening process far removed from the spiritual contemplation we usually think of as the sole occupation of monks; such training may well have helped mold his fearless character, and we know that by the time he reached early manhood, he was much admired for his physical strength. But in leading his rebellion, he restrained the peasantry from mass pillage, thereby gaining the support of the upper classes and uniting his country in a successful effort to drive out the Mongols. Triumphantly, Chu Yüan-chang founded the Ming dynasty, the next-to-the-last Chinese royal house, and took the title of Hung-wu as its first emperor.

THE MING DYNASTY:
Time of Connoisseurs and Collectors

In his reign Hung-wu made Nanking his capital, but his son Yung-lo, the strongest Ming emperor, later moved his capital to Peking to be nearer the threatened northern frontier in case the dreaded Mongol, Tamerlane, chose to invade China. He reinforced the earthen Great Wall with stone to protect northern China. He designed Peking on much the same plans that exist today. The city was actually built during the Ch'ing dynasty.

Peking consists of the Imperial City and, within it, the Forbidden City, which was then filled with courts and reception halls, terraces, shrines, meticulously groomed gardens, and reflecting stretches of water.

137. Gate of Supreme Harmony, Forbidden City, Peking (Ch'ing).

138.

139.

Two views of the Imperial Summer Palace outside Peking (Ch'ing).

Outside the Imperial City Yung-lo built the Temple of Heaven, a circular temple resting on three marble terraces. It is a masterpiece of Chinese architecture. Many more buildings remain from the Ming period than from earlier times—ramparts and gate towers along the Great Wall, temples and pagodas, palaces and royal tombs, which are often large and magnificent (see Plates 137, 138, 139).

The driving ambition of the early Ming emperors was to restore the native traditions and thought of China in all aspects of her civilization. Early in his reign Yung-lo assembled two thousand scholars to undertake a staggering project—an encyclopedia of Chinese knowledge; eventually 11,095 volumes were compiled containing the most important writings of the past on history, government, philosophy, industry, religion, and the arts. Classical education was revived, and the *Five Classics* and *Four Books,* containing the teachings of Confucius, became the foundation of acceptable scholarship. To be given a position in the national civil service, an applicant had to be letter-perfect in his knowledge of these rigid, old-fashioned texts. This did not encourage much originality of ideas, but it did make it possible for a diligent student, no matter what his social rank, to grasp a place for himself in the world of government.

The Ming period was an age of Chinese art collectors and connoisseurs. Yung-lo himself was an ardent admirer of carved lacquer (his enthusiasm was heightened by the discovery that the Japanese would pay small fortunes for the best Chinese examples), and the successors to the Yüan masters were summoned to Peking to open an imperial workshop. No academy of painting was established by the Ming emperors, but favored painters were treated with the greatest respect and given special favors and titles at court. This sort of official recognition was met with polite boredom by artists of true talent and worth, however, as they preferred to concentrate their energies on the beauties of nature, finding their rewards in personal creation and the appreciation of fellow artist-scholars. Highly refined Chinese artists have always had a quiet horror of anything "commissioned," that is to say, any work which has been ordered specifically or paid for in advance. This explains why so very few sculptors or ceramicists working on commissions have had their names recorded for posterity; their artistic achievements were intended less as a means of self-expression than as decorations for a temple or as luxurious objects for a rich man's house.

The most accurate word to describe the Ming court would be "conservative," and we shall notice little that is daringly different in the paintings which found favor. Artists were still energetically encouraged, however, and a number of rulers seriously tried their own hands at painting. Emperor Hsuan-tsung in particular specialized in animals and brought many painters to Peking. The most gifted artist of this period, Tai Chin, died poor and unhonored, but not before he had founded the Chê school of painting. His *Returning Home at Evening in Spring* (Plate 140), which depicts twisted pines, weary workmen, a distant temple, and wooded hills, reminds one of Southern Sung academy paintings, but seems to give more storytelling details of human life than they did. Two painters by the names of Wu Wei and Chang Lu, active in the latter part of the fifteenth century, are the most noted of Tai Chin's followers.

The second major school, Wu, took its name from Wu-hsien near Soochow in the Yangtse River delta, where many of its painters lived. They were mostly amateur painters of the scholar-official class we have come to know and generally chose to live in retirement. They were extremely interested in technique, and constantly practiced and experimented with fine variations of brushstrokes. Shên Chou, the founder of the Wu school, learned to paint by carefully studying the old masters, and at different times he borrowed the styles of the masters Wang Mêng, Ni Tsan, and Wu Chên of

141. *Walking with a Stick,* hanging scroll, ink on paper, by Shên Chou (Ming, 1427–1509).

the Yüan period. His own personal style shows much strength and imagination. His hanging scroll *Walking with a Stick* (Plate 141) looks like a slightly crowded Ni Tsan, but his *Landscape* (Plate 142), in which he has used all manner of tight and free strokes, has a fresh and lively quality, seeming to move about with the natural rhythms of breeze-tossed trees and coursing streams. He often uses pale blue, gray-green, and reddish tan washes, yet the colors are never permitted to detract from the brushwork

140. *Returning Home at Evening in Spring,* hanging scroll, ink and colors on silk, by Tai Chin (Ming).

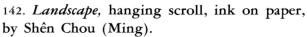

142. *Landscape,* hanging scroll, ink on paper, by Shên Chou (Ming).

143. *The Farewell,* hanging scroll, ink and colors on paper, by Wen Chêng-ming (Ming).

144. *Landscape with Rocks and Mountains,* hanging scroll, ink and light colors on paper, signed by Lu Chih (Ming).

and ink tones. Wen Chêng-ming, another scholar-painter from Soochow, was influenced by Shên Chou but developed a more elegant manner of his own with delicate detail and clear colors, as shown in *The Farewell* (Plate 143). Lu Chih is perhaps the most interesting painter to use the refined style of Wen Chêng-ming, although some critics feel that such works as *Land-*

scape with *Rocks and Mountains* (Plate 144) sacrifice too much strength for the sake of delicacy.

T'ang Yin and Ch'iu Ying, two outstanding Ming painters, do not really belong to the Chê or Wu schools. T'ang Yin's landscapes are his best work, being both realistic and poetic at the same time. In *Fishing in the River in Autumn* (Plate 145), the wooden house thatched with reeds, the boat and figures, the rocks and leaves are all carefully drawn in accurate detail. The sur-

face of the river, ruffled into shallow waves by the breeze, is wonderfully suggested by long, light brushstrokes. T'ang Yin also painted exquisite fans in ink such as the one showing chrysanthemums and bamboo (Plate 146).

Ch'iu Ying, a professional artist, was the last great painter to work in the detailed, lushly colored "blue and green" style dating from the T'ang dynasty. *Saying Farewell at Hsün-yang* (Plate 147) is typical of his long, fascinatingly detailed scrolls, while

146. **Fan with chrysanthemums and bamboo, ink and colors on paper, by T'ang Yin (Ming).**

145. *Fishing in the River in Autumn,* hand scroll, ink and colors on silk, by T'ang Yin (Ming).

Waiting for the Ferry in Autumn (Plate 148) reveals him in a different, subdued mood, using soft, subtle colors to suggest the misty atmosphere of fall.

Tung Ch'i-ch'ang, considered the best late Ming painter, worked in a style that seems startlingly "modern" and simplified, especially when compared with that of one of his contemporaries, Ku Itze, whose *Mountain Valley* (Plate 149) could not be more traditional. Tung Ch'i-ch'ang's *Mountain Landscape* (Plate 150) seems to take an almost childlike approach to nature, but this in fact is not true; his paintings are very carefully designed, and certain forms are repeated, in this case peaks, to create a unified overall pattern.

Carefully planned decorative compositions were used to illustrate books of poetry; more sumptuous than the kind of illustration we are accustomed to, Ch'ên Hung-shou's illustration for T'ao Yüan-ming's poem "The Homecoming" (Plate 151) was painted on silk. This masterful work also shows us Chinese materials for painting and calligraphy spread out on the stone before the seated figure.

148. *Waiting for the Ferry in Autumn,* hanging scroll, ink and colors on silk, marked with the seal of Ch'iu Ying (Ming).

Glowing color and incredibly elaborate decoration returned to the "applied" arts of lacquer work, jade carving, porcelain making, etc. Lacquer furniture—cabinets and caskets painted or inlaid with mother-of-pearl—was produced in the Ming (or the

147. *Saying Farewell at Hsün-yang,* hand scroll, ink and colors on paper, by Ch'iu Ying (Ming).

Ch'ing) period for export. These magnificent objects were to influence permanently European tastes in interior decoration. Three examples are to be seen in Plates 152, 153, and 154. The first, a traveling chest in red-lacquered wood, is incised and inlaid in red, black, and gold with pairs of dragons, suns, and clouds. The second is a stupendous cabinet in black-lacquered wood inlaid with mother-of-pearl and gold lacquer, and the designs include everything from landscapes and calligraphy to dragons and still lifes. The lacquered cabinet with raised dragons and clouds in Plate 154 is decorated with a gold-dust-and-lacquer process that Chinese craftsmen learned from the Japan-

149. *Mountain Valley,* hanging scroll, ink on paper, by Ku Itze (1628).

150. *Mountain Landscape,* album painting, ink and colors on paper, Tung Ch'i-ch'ang (Late Ming).

151. Illustration for the poem "The Homecoming," hand scroll, ink and light colors on silk, by Ch'ên Hung-shou (Ming).

152. Traveling chest in red-lacquered wood (Ming, 1613).

ese. The jade-topped incense burner in Plate 155 was executed by a craftsman, or craftsmen, with a superb sense of design and infinite patience. It would be impossible to estimate the number of coats of lacquer which must have been tediously applied to achieve a thickness that could be so deeply carved.

In jade carving Ming craftsmen developed an ornate, pictorial style which was certainly new; the figures they made lost all their ritual meaning and became precious collec-

153. Cabinet in black-lacquered wood inlaid with mother-of-pearl and gold lacquer (Ch'ing, early eighteenth century).

154. Lacquered cabinet with raised decoration in gold (Late Ming or Early Ch'ing).

tors' objects. Another splendid decorative figure is the small-scale wooden sculpture of Kuan-yin, Goddess of Mercy, seen in Plate 156.

Despite the high quality of these decorative arts, it is for the excellence of its porcelain that the Ming dynasty is most renowned. Ching-tê Chen, always a center for the production of porcelain, became an imperial center in the fifteenth century. In this district in northeast Kiangsai were found the minerals needed for making porcelain. An imperial factory was built there to keep the court supplied with porcelain. From then on Ching-tê Chen dominated the art of porcelain making in China.

Chinese artisans would let their wares dry in the air and would glaze them and then fire them all at once. The shimmering surface makes the colors of the porcelain look like beautiful and brilliant stones lying under crystal-clear water. Mohammedan cobalt blue, imported from Persia, was generally used in the famous blue-and-white porcelain. Most of this porcelain dates from the sixteenth and seventeenth centuries. When painting was not used, the decoration was carved, incised, or molded before glazing. Different-colored glazes were kept apart by ridges, as in the flower-strewn porcelain vase in Plate 157. This is also an example of *mei-p'ing,* or plum blossom type of vase. The blue-and-white vase in Plate 158 bears an elaborate design of three gentlemen playing checkers in a fantastic garden. Another typical blue-and-white Ming porcelain is the 'pilgrim flask' with dragon, flowers, and birds in Plate 159, which was made for export to the Persian market.

After blue-and-white, the largest class of Ming porcelain is that glazed in two or more colors. These "overglazes" can be enamels fired with glass and colored green, yellow, turquoise, or purple with metallic oxides, or else they may be the "iron red" and brownish black tones derived from manganese. In Plate 160 the pattern of flying dragons has been filled in with green enamel after application of the orange glaze to the rest of the body. The porcelain stem-cup in Plate 161 is quite rare; the red underglaze decoration is meant to represent a fruit, either a litchi or a pomegranate. The beautiful porcelain dish in Plate 162 is decorated

155. Incense burner in carved lacquer with jade top (Ming).

156. Figurine of Kuan-yin in wood (Ming).

157. *Mei-p'ing* porcelain vase (Ming)

158. Blue-and-white porcelain vase with gentlemen playing checkers (Ming).

in five colors with a lovely pattern of leaves, flowers, and a bird, all within an eight-sided frame.

The Ming dynasty ended with the Manchus, Mongolian inhabitants of Manchuria, storming across the northern border and seizing the throne. It was the same old sad story. After a healthy, productive period of expanding power a strong dynasty stopped producing competent rulers and the central government lost its grip. The backbone of the empire was viciously broken by insurrections, palace jealousies, and general national dissatisfactions of one sort or another. Finally, a new dynasty was established, the Ch'ing in this case, which then ironically tried to reconstruct the world of the preceding rulers.

Since the late sixteenth century the Manchus, living to the northeast of China with their capital at Mukden, had been a poten-

160. Glazed porcelain vase decorated with enamel (Ming).

161. Porcelain stem-cup (Ming).

159. Pilgrim flask in porcelain (Ming).

162. **Porcelain dish in five colors (Ming).**

tially dangerous power. When rebellion against Ming rule broke out in 1644, a Chinese general asked the Manchu ruler to help him regain Peking. The results of this invitation were hardly what he had anticipated: A Manchu army occupied Peking and stayed. It took the Manchus forty years to subdue all of China. Their numbers were insignificant compared with China's teeming population, but they more than made up for this deficiency through sheer craftiness. Rather than rejecting Chinese traditions, the Manchus sensibly professed a deep respect and admiration for them, thereby winning over the mandarin class, those who had passed the Confucian civil service examinations. The Manchus were less destructive than the Mongols, and tried in every way to preserve Chinese systems of government and society without change. The *Five Classics* and *Four Books* were preserved, and the Confucian examinations on these ancient texts were continued. This conservative

policy succeeded until foreign intrusions and rebellions led to loss of territory and a weakening of the dynasty in the nineteenth century.

The Ch'ing period was an interesting and extremely active one for the arts, especially during the reigns of the most renowned Ch'ing emperors, K'ang-hsi (1662–1722), Yung-chên (1723–1735), and Ch'ien-lung (1736–1795). It was an age of research, preservation of ancient texts, and the collecting of bronzes and paintings. The wasteful and extravagant Emperor Ch'ien-lung constantly added to his own vast collections by impulsively buying up private ones. His fickle interests kept his court in permanent confusion. He loved technical tricks like curious clocks and intricately plotted fountains. He could paint passably well and also counted himself a writer which was responsible for his unfortunate habit of writing reams of poetry over other artists' far superior scrolls.

There was no great change in the manner of painting after the fall of the Ming. A variety of styles existed for painters to follow, and many painters often worked in several different ones. But the best Ch'ing painters worked in their own individual way, which the weight of tradition could not suffocate.

In the late seventeenth and early eighteenth centuries the most important and unified group of artists followed the teaching of Tung Ch'i-ch'ang (see Plate 150). He believed that the painter should try not merely to reproduce the outward appearance of nature, but also to express his inner feelings about it. The Ch'ing painters studied and copied the old masters, especially the Yüan landscape painters, as Tung Ch'i-ch'ang recommended, hoping in this way to discover their technical secrets and essential approach to art. Through these outward techniques they strove to perfect their ability to express their inner feelings.

They were less interested in what was painted than in the way it was presented. They concentrated on such painters' problems as the grouping and balancing of shapes, and on brushstrokes which would most effectively create form, structure, and tone. The artists who most faithfully followed this rather overly intellectual approach to painting were, as might be expected, of the scholar-official class.

One of these men, Wang Shih-min, a pupil of Tung Ch'i-ch'ang, passed on his ideas to younger painters, together with the high technical standards of the Ming. His lovely wintry hanging scroll, *Landscape* (Plate 163), clearly shows a strong Yüan influence on his style of interpreting the natural world. Wang Chien, whose *Mountain Landscape* is seen in Plate 164, was another government official, and a very competent painter in the Ch'ing version of Yüan landscape styles. He sometimes painted albums of ten or twelve pages in which each landscape was an interpretation of an old master. These albums were highly prized in the Ch'ing period.

Wang Hui studied with Wang Shih-min and painted in a wide variety of styles. But by the time he reached full maturity as an artist, he had developed his own very distinctive style, which can be seen in *Landscape with Mountains and Forests* (Plate 165). In this painting, dots are used to suggest low-growing vegetation, and the rough "hemp-fiber" brushstroke suggests the forms of weathered hills and rocks.

Yet it was Wang Yüan-ch'i, the youngest of these four painters (who, though unrelated, came to be known as the "Four Wangs"), who proved to be the most original of them all. Wang Yüan-ch'i, a distinguished scholar and civil servant, painted in a style that is more difficult and compli-

163. *Landscape,* hanging scroll, ink on paper, by **Wang Shih-min (Early Ch'ing).**

cated than it appears to be at first sight. In *Landscape in the Style of Tung Ch'i-ch'ang* (Plate 166), the large area of bluish off-white becomes both sky and lake, and the brilliantly conceived landmass is treated as one detailed and fascinating shape.

Wu Li, a close friend of Wang Hui, chose to paint pictures in the Yüan tradition, such

165. *Landscape with Mountains and Forests,* ink and colors on paper, by Wang Hui (Ch'ing).

164. *Mountain Landscape,* hanging scroll, ink and colors on paper, by Wang Chien (Ch'ing).

166. *Landscape in the Style of Tung Ch'i-ch'ang,* hanging scroll, ink and colors on paper, by Wang Yüan-ch'i (Ch'ing).

as *Landscape in the Style of Ni Tsan* (Plate 167), which in this particular instance recalls the works of the earlier master through the use of pale tones in dry ink and a composition that includes sparse and leafless trees clinging to rocky ground, and a meandering expanse of lake. The bold upper masses of rock and mountains, however, are introduced as Wu Li's own personal touch.

Other Ch'ing artists refused to be bound to the "glorious past" and struck out in their own directions. Kung Hsien, the outstanding painter of a group known as the Eight Masters of Chinling, worked in a highly personal way and created an extraordinary range of tones and patterns. A solitary person, he painted the same subjects over and over again throughout his life. In his typical *River Landscape* (Plate 168), he painted rocks with short strokes of a dry brush, then used wet ink and dots to shade and model them.

Hung-jên, who became a Buddhist monk with the fall of the Ming dynasty, was also influenced by Ni Tsan. However, his hanging scrolls, such as *The Coming of Autumn* (Plate 169), have the magical fragility of a fairy-tale crystal palace. In sharp contrast to the unsurpassed delicacy of Hung-jên's paintings are the bold expressionistic scenes of Chu-ta, the strongest of the individualists, whose works today seem amazingly modern. He used blank spaces like the Southern Sung masters, as, for instance, in *River Landscape* (Plate 170). *Mountain Landscape* (Plate 171), with its blunt outlines and surging sense of life, reminds one of Cézanne, a famous French painter of the nineteenth century.

The last great age of Chinese porcelain came during the reigns of K'ang-hsi, Yung-chên, and Ch'ien-lung and extended from 1662 to 1795. These emperors supported the imperial factory at Ching-tê Chen, and

their officials were its managing directors. In sheer technical skill and decorative artistry Ch'ing ceramics are supreme throughout the world, and there was an enormous demand for this magnificently colored, imaginative ware in Europe and America during the eighteenth and nineteenth centuries. The range of techniques is very wide.

Underglaze blue was still used, but with different tones and a new brilliance (see Plate 172). Porcelains with overglazes of enamel painting are known by names invented by the French art historian Jacquemart in the nineteenth century: *famille verte, famille noire,* and *famille rose,* meaning the green, black, and rose families, respectively. In the first, green is the dominating color of the color scheme. Earlier simple designs of birds and flowers were replaced in the eighteenth century by landscapes; everyday-life, or "genre," scenes; and illustrations to romantic tales often taken from prints. The porcelain *rouleau,* or rolled, vase in Plate 173 is lavishly painted with such an illustration. *Famille noire* porcelain is so called because black is the dominant background color, but it really is a variation of *famille verte,* since the enamel overglaze is green (see Plate 174). *Famille rose* porcelain was made entirely for export; its characteristic delicate rose-pink shade may be seen in the fragile flower to the left on an enchanting little vase standing only two inches high (Plate 175). Blanc de chine ("white of china") was greatly favored by foreign collectors. This fine white porcelain was first made in the late Ming period, and its production went on into the twentieth century. Perfect use of its superbly lustrous qualities may be appreciated in an exquisite statuette of Kuan-yin (Plate 176). Another ornament with a great appeal is the *famille verte* "Dog of Fo" in Plate 177, a mythical animal originally sculpted in pairs as guardians for use either at the gate of a Buddhist

167. *Landscape in the Style of Ni Tsan,* hanging scroll, ink on paper, by Wu Li (Ch'ing).

169. *The Coming of Autumn,* hanging scroll, ink on paper, by Hung-jên (Ch'ing).

temple or on each side of a statue of Buddha. The ceramic animals are seldom more than twelve inches high.

Lacquer work lost none of the splendor of the Ming period. The small cupboard

168. *River Landscape,* hand scroll, ink on paper, by Kung Hsien (Ch'ing).

170. *River Landscape,* album painting, ink and colors on silk, by Chu-ta (Ch'ing).

171. *Mountain Landscape,* album painting, ink and colors on silk, by Chu-ta (Ch'ing).

172. Porcelain ginger jar with cover (Ch'ing).

173. *Famille verte* porcelain *rouleau* vase (Ch'ing).

174. *Famille noire* porcelain vase with overglaze enamel painting (Ch'ing).

175. Miniature porcelain vase (Ch'ing).

178. Cupboard in lacquered wood (Ch'ing).

176. Blanc de chine statue of Kuan-yin (Ch'ing).

177. "Dog of Fo," *famille verte* porcelain statuette (Ch'ing).

84

179. **Throne of Emperor Ch'ien-lung, in carved red lacquer inlaid with gold (Ch'ing).**

in Plate 178, inlaid with mother-of-pearl, jade, and semiprecious stones and fitted with gilt bronze, has the brilliance of a painting. The spectacular red-and-gold throne created for the luxury-loving Emperor Ch'ien-lung (Plate 179) shows lacquer carving at its absolute peak of craftsmanship and ornateness. It is precisely this sort of Chinese imperial and artistic magnificence which will continue to enthrall generations of history and art students throughout the world.

Chinese art spans the greatest length of time of all the world's cultures. Throughout their history, until most recent times, the Chinese have adhered to one tradition. They remained faithful to values of their ancestors; they have kept close to the age-old attitudes toward art, involving love of nature, purity of feeling, calmness, and serenity. They have even retained the same motifs and techniques introduced centuries ago, and within this tradition they perfected the arts of their ancestors, which are among the greatest in the world.

Korea

KOREA WAS DEEPLY influenced by Chinese culture, but this did not prevent Korean artists and craftsmen from making their own original and distinctive contribution to art. The position of the Korean peninsula makes it inevitable that, throughout her history, Korea should be linked with the great civilizations of China and Japan. The map on page 87 (Plate 180) shows the chief cultural centers of the country, and the chart below lists the major periods of her history.

Three Kingdoms	57 B.C.–A.D. 668
Koguryo—	37 B.C.–A.D. 668
Paekche—	18 B.C.–A.D. 663
Silla—	57 B.C.–A.D. 668
Great Silla Kingdom	A.D. 668–A.D. 935
Koryo Kingdom	A.D. 918–A.D. 1392
Yi Kingdom	A.D. 1392–A.D. 1910

181. Gold belt buckle, probably of Chinese workmanship (second century B.C.).

During the second century B.C., the Chinese Han dynasty ruled part of the Korean peninsula, and the large, well-preserved site of one of the Han colonies was discovered at Lo-lang by a Japanese expedition in 1909. Hundreds of tombs were unearthed, and in them were found mirrors and weapons, lacquer objects, pottery, and ritual jades. A beautiful granulated-gold belt buckle studded with turquoise (Plate 181) was among the long-buried works of art. Most of the objects probably had come from China, however, and the find was principally significant in that it clearly proved the close contact between that country and Korea.

In the first century B.C. the Three Kingdoms arose in Korea. These states were constantly at war for seven hundred years, during which time Buddhism reached

Korea, in 372 A.D. It became the official religion of the Koguryo rulers, who maintained relations with the Buddhist Tartars of northern Wei in China. The art of Koguryo survives in mural paintings of processions, hunting scenes, and human and mythological figures that were found in tombs around Pyong-yang and Tungkou. The Paekche kingdom developed its own individual Buddhist art, inspired by Wei sculpture. Paekche was the link between Chinese and Japanese Buddhism, and craftsmen from Paekche settled in Japan in 577 A.D. Northern Wei sculptural influence can be identified in a gilt-bronze Buddha Amitābha (Plate 182). The basic design of smoke and flames rising from rounded mountain peaks used in a Paekche terra-cotta tomb slab (Plate 183) might put one in mind of a Chinese "hill jar" incense burner, but the resemblance is slight.

The Silla kingdom finally emerged as the most powerful of the three early states. Compact and centralized, it was further endowed with fertile soil, minerals, and an industrious people. With the help of the T'ang armies, it defeated the other two kingdoms and remained independent, ruling Korea from 668 A.D. to 935 A.D., the Great Silla period. Among the most interesting finds of the early Silla culture are openwork metal ornaments, jewelry, images and pendants meant to ward off evil spirits, and a pure gold crown, all from tombs near Kyongju. A fired clay vessel in the form of a warrior on horseback (the same sturdy type as the Chou horses) came from the

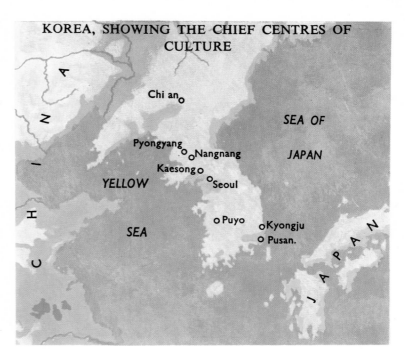

180. Map showing chief cultural centers of Korea.

182. The Buddha Amitābha, Northern Wei Buddhist sculpture, gilt-bronze (577 A.D.).

183. Terra-cotta tomb slab (seventh century A.D.).

Tomb of the Golden Bell at Kyongju, as did a gray pottery ritual lamp with five cupped oil containers (Plates 184, 185).

The Great Silla was a creative period that saw the unification of the Korean language, but wars and invasions have destroyed its greatest works of art. The most important remains are the ruins of a temple at Pulguk-sa and of the cave temple of Sukkulam in the nearby hills. Of the shrine of Pulguk-sa, a stone stairway and balustrade, pagodas, and two bronze images are all that remain to suggest its original beauty. Sukkulam has fared much better; a large central statue of a seated Buddha still presides over the granite-lined walls bearing twenty-seven carved reliefs of noble bodhisattvas, kings, guardians, and lohans. The fragment of a lokapala, or guardian king, attended by a lion, from a Buddhist temple near Kyongju (Plate 186), shows the shallow-relief style of the Great Silla period. Buddhist ritual

185. Gray pottery ritual oil lamp (fifth or sixth century A.D.).

184. Vessel in form of warrior on horseback, fired clay (Early Silla).

186. Fragment of terra-cotta relief showing lokapala attended by lion (Great Silla, seventh century A.D.).

demanded cremation rather than burial (a Great Silla funeral urn in glazed stoneware with lid and handle appears in Plate 187). The great bronze Korean temple bells of the period were celebrated throughout the breadth of the Eastern world. Occasionally Buddhist images have turned up in the course of explorations at ancient temple sites; these include a seventh century gilt-bronze statue, thought to be authentically Korean, of the Buddha Maitreya (Plate 188), a wooden statue of Yokasa Youra, the bodhisattva of healing (Plate 189), and a gilt-bronze dark-haired statue of Bhaisajya-guru, Master of Medicine (Plate 190).

The reign of Queen Chinsong (887–897 A.D.) paved the way for the collapse of the Silla. Luxury at court had reached such an ostentatious level that the peasantry became not only resentful but outraged. Some enlisted in rebellious bands, and it was the lieutenant of one of these, Wang Kon, who finally wrested the country from the Silla. He founded the Koryo kingdom in 918, and by 935 the Great Silla period was over. He did not seek bloody revenge against the fallen Silla, and in fact went so far as to let his daughter marry their last king.

Under the Koryo rulers, Korea thrived economically and artistically. Beautiful objects were cast in bronze, gold, and silver, and architects were kept busy designing monasteries, pagodas, and palaces. Nevertheless, it was in the field of ceramics that Korean craftsmen excelled to the highest degree. The glaze techniques used in T'ang and Sung ware were imported from China and became responsible for the birth of the great Koryo ceramic ware. The glaze, composed mainly of iron oxide, produced a range of colors, including yellow, blue, and gray-green, or celadon. The most sought-after was the celadon pale green, which resembled

187. Funeral urn in glazed stoneware (Great Silla, eighth to ninth centuries A.D.).

188. Gilt-bronze statue of the Buddha Maitreya (seventh century A.D.).

190. Gilt-bronze statue of Bhaisajyaguru, Master of Medicine (eighth to ninth centuries A.D.).

189. Wooden statue of Yokasa Youra, the bodhisattva of healing (eighth to ninth centuries A.D.).

natural stone and was prized more highly than silver, the most valuable metal at the time. Bowls, teapots, gourd- and melon-shaped pitchers, headrests, and incense burners were made of this celadon ware. The first examples were totally plain, but later the pieces were adorned with incised lines, low relief, and inlaid in such decorative motifs as peonies, asters, lotus flowers, and flying cranes (see Plates 191 through 194).

The Yi kingdom was founded by a shrewd military man and statesman named Yi Taejo, who overthrew the Koryo in 1392. For a while its potters produced a fine pure-white ware used at court during the fifteenth century (see Plate 195), but after blue-and-white Ming porcelain appeared in Korea, they quickly adopted the new fashion. Hideyoshi, a destructive Japanese warlord, invaded in 1592, and in the ensuing six years he had the major body of Korean art, literature, and architecture destroyed. Korean potters emigrated or were carried off bodily to Japan and resettled on the island of Kyushu; one type of their pottery became famous as the "Ido bowls" used in Japanese tea ceremonies.

Korean paintings date from the Yi period,

with few exceptions. The earliest example included here, *Portrait of a Monk* (Plate 196), with its bold outlines building a formal pattern, its dignity, and its strong colors, recalls the portrait of the Ch'an Buddhist master Wu-Chün (Plate 98). But Buddhism, and the style of the Ch'an Buddhists, was not in favor; the Yi intellectuals were Confucian scholars who imposed strict rules on painting. Fortunately, the artistic spirit can never be completely crushed, and by the seventeenth century, artists of original talent had found new inspiration in the Korean landscape. The first of these, Chong Son, broke away from the restrictions of Confucian brushwork, if not from the disci-

191. Melon-shaped celadon pitcher (eleventh to twelfth centuries A.D.).

192. Flask in painted celadon ware (eleventh to twelfth centuries A.D.).

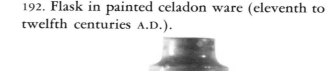

194. Celadon vase of *mei-p'ing* type, inlaid with "Thousand Cranes" design.

193. Shallow celadon bowl, inlaid with lotus flower and aster pattern (twelfth century A.D.).

195. Yi wine jar in white porcelain with underglaze painting of vine leaves and grapes (seventeenth to eighteenth centuries A.D.).

196. *Portrait of a Monk,* colors on silk (Yi, fourteenth century A.D.).

pline and techniques of Chinese landscape painters. Hyônjae Sim Sajong and Tanwôn Kim Hong-do carried on in this individual style (see Plates 197, 198). Tanwôn Kim Hong-do and Hyewôn Sin Yun-bok branched out into genre painting, as, for instance, in Hyewôn Sin Yun-bok's charming and carefully grouped *Concert on the River* (Plate 199). A genuinely Korean style and character was developed in lively studies of wild and domestic animals. A fine example of the Korean genius in this field is Hyônjae

Sim Sajong's stealthy, bristling tiger (Plate 200), whose fur is so realistic one feels he might stroke it, if he dared.

Korean art developed under several handicaps. The small country was surrounded by China and Japan, both much larger and stronger nations. The Korean artists were certainly strongly influenced by the art of China. However, they developed an artistic viewpoint of their own, and produced a great deal of original work which was to have its own influence on the art of Japan.

199. *Concert on the River,* album painting, ink and colors on paper, by Hyewôn Sin Yun-bok (eighteenth century).

200. Hanging scroll depicting tiger, ink and colors on paper, by Hyônjae Sim Sajong (eighteenth century).

197. *Landscape in Rain,* hanging scroll, ink and colors on paper, by Hyônjae Sim Sajong (eighteenth century).

198. *Rocks in the Sea,* hanging scroll by Tanwôn Kim Hong-do (eighteenth century).

Japan

TOO FREQUENTLY, when people speak in terms of "Oriental art," they make the great error of assuming that the civilizations of China and Japan developed in the same stately and leisurely way. This is a totally unfounded assumption, for the civilization of China begins several thousand years before that of Japan. The lengthy period preceding 552 A.D., regarded as Japan's legendary or prehistoric age, is divided into the Jōmon and Yayoi periods. The latter part of the Yayoi period is also known as the Yameto, or Great Burial, period.

The culture of the Jōmon, a nomadic hunting and fishing people, apparently had its first origins in eastern Japan and later fanned out northward. From this dim and remote age a number of pottery figurines of human beings or fertility gods have survived, along with a few vessels made by the coiled clay method; the name "Jōmon" actually means "coiled rope." The tense, powerfully modeled figures seem to be the work of an imaginative society dominated by a fearful belief in supernatural forces. The figures are meant to be viewed from the front and, although simply modeled, sometimes bear elaborate surface decorations. Four different specimens appear in Plates 202 through 205. Their exact meaning remains a mystery, but it is generally thought that they must have served a symbolic or religious purpose.

In the third century B.C., the Yayoi culture, named after a suburb of Tokyo where the first discoveries of it were made, replaced the Jōmon; their relics are so different from those we have just seen that it seems a new people must have invaded Japan and gradually forced out the older, more primitive

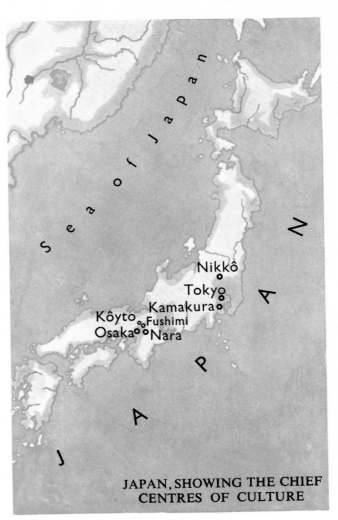

JAPAN, SHOWING THE CHIEF CENTRES OF CULTURE

201. Map showing chief cultural centers of Japan.

JAPAN FROM PREHISTORIC TIMES TO MODERN TIMES

Prehistoric period	until A.D. 552
Jōmon and Yayoi	
Asuka period	A.D. 552–645
Nara period	645–784
Heian period	784–1185
Early Heian	784–897
Middle & Late Heian, or Fujiwara	897–1185
Kamakura period	1185–1333
Muromachi period	1333–1573
Momoyama period	1573–1614
Edo, or Tokugawa period	1614–1868
Meiji Restoration	1868–
(modern times)	

94

202.

204.

203.

205.

Statuettes in pottery (Jōmon).

culture. We have no clear picture of the Yayoi until after the end of the second century A.D., when the outlines of an agricultural society emerge; at first the Yayoi were probably grouped in tribes, and later in a series of small states.

The practice of burying kings or important men in tombs surrounded by massive mounds gave the Great Burial period its name. The custom was introduced after the second century A.D. The largest tomb, which took forty years to build, is that of Emperor Nintoku (*c.* 400 A.D.); it stands ninety feet high and, including its moat, covers eighty acres. Arranged around these tombs were · clay cylinders called *haniwa*, "circles in clay"; other *haniwa* might be grouped together on top of the mound. Some are nothing more than simple cylinders; others are either crowned with a figure, like that of the alert, uncertain hen in Plate 206, or are more freely modeled on cylindrical legs like the horse in Plate 207. These *haniwa* vary from twenty to forty inches in height and may take the forms of animals, humans, or even houses. *Haniwa* craftsmen obviously studied their subjects thoroughly and modeled their animals with sympathetic understanding of their basic characteristics; this is pointed out not only by the nervous hen but also by a hauntingly sad little clay monkey (Plate 208).

The pottery tomb guardians, such as the *haniwa* warrior in Plate 209, tell us a great deal about the society of the Great Burial period. From them we deduce that a powerful warrior class existed, and that metalwork was sufficiently advanced for the making of swords and the forging and riveting of helmets. Native craftsmen made decorated bell-shaped objects called *dotaku* and also cast bronze mirrors so similar to established Chinese examples that the Japanese plainly must have had some contact with the mainland.

209. *Haniwa* warrior with helmet, pottery (Yayoi).

Ordinary men and women, as well as warriors, appear in *haniwa* figures. Both men and women were important in the private household, and it was natural that on a man's death he should be guarded by those people to whom he had been close during his lifetime. The man in the ballooning trousers and something very akin to a

208. *Haniwa* monkey in clay (fifth to sixth centuries A.D.).

206. *Haniwa* hen in clay (fifth to sixth centuries A.D.).

207. *Haniwa* horse (Yayoi).

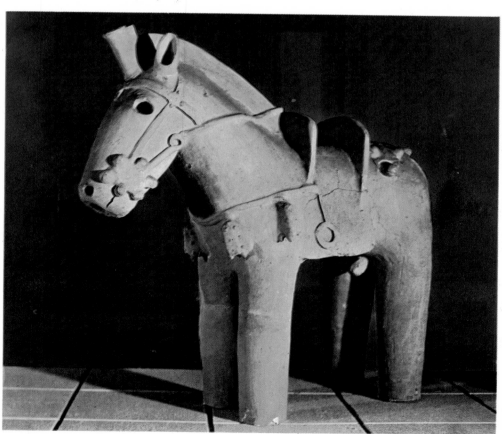

211. *Haniwa* woman in decorated dress, pottery
(Yayoi).

210. *Haniwa* figure of a man, pottery (Yayoi).

bowler hat (Plate 210) probably represented a relative or high-ranking servant. The woman (Plate 211), a rarer figure, wears a soft beret-like cap and what appears to be a print dress. Their stiff, arms-akimbo stances are typical; so is the way their features, particularly the hollowed eyes and slit mouths, are indicated, not much differently from those of the monkey. The resulting expressions are very much like caricatures and seem a special accomplishment of the Japanese artist.

As we have seen, many Korean craftsmen arrived in Japan during the sixth century A.D. Contact with Korea, established during the Yayoi period, possibly as early as the first century A.D., became closer as time passed; therefore the Japanese were probably quite aware of Buddhism well before its establishment in their own country. It is conveniently agreed upon by most historians of the Orient that the date 552 A.D. was a most significant one for Japan; in this year the Korean king of Paekche sent, with the approval of the Japanese authorities, a gift of Buddhist scriptures and a gilt-bronze Buddha image to the Japanese Emperor Kimmei, thereby bringing about the subsequent conversion of the court. Examining the situation more realistically, we must admit that it took at least fifty years of innumerable political squabbles between violently disagreeing groups for Buddhism to become firmly entrenched. At first the warlords and local chieftains opposed it, thinking their powers would be diminished; others did not want to be torn from their old gods and faith. But the forward-thinking faction recognized the superiority of the highly organized civilizations of Korea and China; it was they who tirelessly championed the adoption of Buddhism as a means of national development. They were proved right. With the final triumph of Buddhism,

new and important contacts with Asia, especially China, were cemented. These in turn changed Japanese standards of living and stimulated the country's intellectual life. Patronage of Buddhist art developed, inspiring sculptors and painters and providing them with an entirely new viewpoint.

Prince Shōtoku Taishi (574–622 A.D.), who reigned for his aunt, the Empress Suiko, might be regarded as the official founder of Buddhism in Japan. During the first half of the Asuka period (which extended, in full, from 552 to 645 A.D.), Japanese sculpture was based indirectly on the Chinese eastern Wei empire style, or more directly on Korean models. Early in the seventh century, after the founding of the T'ang dynasty in China, Prince Shōtoku Taishi sent envoys and monks to China to study and trade. They were staggered by what they saw. Through them, the splendors of T'ang culture began to reach Japan before the end of the Asuka period and gradually penetrated all levels of society.

The official recognition of Buddhism naturally resulted in a desire to build temples. As with religious sculpture, Chinese and Korean examples were used as models. One of the most beautiful results, reverently preserved through the centuries, is the Kondō ("Buddha Hall") and pagoda of Hōryūji, built in the time of Prince Shōtoku Taishi (Plates 212, 213). A fascinating decoration that originally hung from a roof beam at Hōryūji is a fifteen-foot gilt-bronze "banner"; a detail, showing a flute player and a dancer, is shown in Plate 214.

Under the patronage of Prince Shōtoku Taishi, a sculptor named Tori and his followers represented the Chinese tradition in Japanese sculpture at the height of the Asuka period, in the early seventh century. The sculptors of the Korean tradition are not known by name, and few examples of their

212. Kondō of Hōryūji near Nara (seventh century).

213. Pagoda of Hōryūji near Nara (seventh century).

214. Detail of a gilt-bronze "banner" (Asuka).

work survive. One such is the Kudara Kwannon (Plate 215), which, with the exception of the hands and scarves, is carved from a single piece of camphorwood. "Kwannon" is the Japanese name for Avalokitésvara, Lord of Compassion; like his Chinese counterpart Kuan-yin, he eventually changed sexes and became the goddess of mercy. "Kudara" was the Japanese name for the Korean kingdom of Paekche. This figure, greatly elongated, shows little attempt to create an effect of volume. Nor does the figure of Miroku, Buddha of the Future (Plate 216), who is supposed to appear thousands of years after the Buddha's entry into nirvana. He is shown here with one leg raised, in the pose called *hanka;* the figure differs from most others like it in that it is carved in pine rather than camphorwood and wears a coronet instead of a topknot of hair. In any case, it does typify the sexless quality of the major figures in the Buddhist art of China and Japan. The same *hanka* position is taken by another figure of the Future Buddha (Plate 217), which is almost unequaled in Japanese sculpture for its smooth surface planes and lustrous, dignified elegance.

Tori, believed to be the grandson of a Chinese immigrant, founded a school of sculpture in the Nara region while working for Prince Shōtoku Taishi, for whose "repose" a Shaka triad (Buddha Sākyāmuni and two bodhisattvas, Plate 218) was cast in 623 A.D., the prince having died the previous year. The outlined patterns of the robes, and the halo and the larger aureole (an encircling ring of light), seem more important than the figures. A figure of Yakushi, Buddha of Medicine (Plate 219), attributed to Tori, is almost identically draped, and the aureole behind him bears the same motif of seven tiny Buddhas. The style of bronze sculpture in the Asuka period leans heavily

on the one established at Lung-mên in China in the early sixth century. The frontality of the figures and the proportions—long heads and faces dominating short bodies—are typical (see Plates 220 and 221). Later in the seventh century, the strong lines of the drapery became less formal and the postures slightly more relaxed, although the heads and hands remained large (see Plate 222). An Amida triad (Plate 223) shows a marked change in the style of physical proportion and is a good example of the transition from Asuka to the Nara style of the eighth century. Amida is the Japanese Buddha of Boundless Light, otherwise termed Amitābha.

The Nara period, named after the great new capital city to which the court moved

215. **Carved statue of Kudara Kwannon, camphorwood (seventh century).**

216. Carved statue of Miroku, pine wood (Asuka).

218. Shaka triad sculpture, by Tori (dated 623).

217. **Figure of Miroku, Buddha of the Future, wood (Asuka).**

in 710 A.D., began around 645 A.D. with the "Taika reforms" and the subsequent introduction of a largely accepted Chinese political and administrative system. The Japanese enthusiastically set to work building Nara as a frank imitation of China's vast Ch'ang-an. Today, virtually nothing remains of the city, which was never really completed. The project was just too big an undertaking; after all, Ch'ang-an's population was about two million, or approximately one-third of all Japan's. A curious fact concerning early Japanese capitals is that they were moved after an emperor's death

219. Yakushi, Buddha of Medicine, bronze sculpture, attributed to Tori (seventh century).

220. Shaka Nyorai, gilt-bronze sculpture (early seventh century).

222. Sculptured bodhisattva, in late stage of Asuka style (seventh century).

because the site was then considered defiled.

The transfer of the capital from Fujiwara to Nara, at the northern end of the Yamato plain (see map on page 94, Plate 201), in 710 A.D. is an event of particular architectural importance in the development of Japanese civilization. New temples and monasteries seemed to shoot up overnight. Buildings varied in size from the restrained Yumedono ("Hall of Dreams"), shown in Plate 224, to the grandiose temple of Tōdaiji, of which little now remains. However, the much-restored Great Buddha (Daibutsu) still dominates the rather badly altered Hall

224. Yumedono ("Hall of Dreams"), Hōryūji, near Nara (eighth century).

221. Sculptured bodhisattva, beginning of late Nara style (seventh century).

223. Amida triad, sculpture (late seventh century).

225. The Hall of the Great Buddha of Tōdaiji, Nara (dedicated in 752).

226. Detail of a bronze lantern (eighth century).

227. The Nikko Bosatsu, clay (dated 747).

of the Great Buddha, probably the world's largest wooden building (Plate 225). Fifty-three feet high, this Great Buddha was, on May 26, 752, dedicated at a remarkable "eye-opening" ceremony. Wielding a large paintbrush, from which hung streamers clutched by the faithful on the ground far below, Emperor Shōmu scrambled up the colossal image and painted in the eyes himself. In case this was not sufficiently dramatic, he then abdicated and became a monk in the temple's monastery.

In the great court in front of the Hall of the Great Buddha of Tōdaiji temple, there stands a massive lantern with eight open-work screens; a detail (Plate 226) of a celestial musician in floating draperies amid flowers and clouds shows the greatest skill in metalworking. The materials used by Japanese sculptors show greater variation in the late Nara period than at any other time. A simply modeled clay statue of the Nikkō

Bosatsu (Plate 227), one of a series of four figures which now stand in the Hokke-dō of Tōdaiji (Plate 228), flanks the splendid Fūkukenjaku Kwannon (Plate 229), a huge dry-lacquer figure twelve feet high, with eight arms, a gilt-bronze crown, necklaces, and a gleaming aureole. And to be found at Tōshōdaiji temple, just outside Nara, is the powerful hollow-lacquer Rushana Butsu (Plate 230), whose peaceful withdrawal is characteristic of the Nara period (Rushana is the Buddha whose light reaches every corner of the universe), and the ferocious warrior guardian Kongō Rikishi (Plate 231), a vajrapani, meaning "Bearer of the Thunderbolt." The great number of guardian figures in Buddhist temples makes individual identification of them extremely difficult.

A similarly frightening clay figure, bearing little evidence of its original paint, is one of twelve life-size guards of the Buddha at Shin Yakushiji (see Plate 232). Other monstrously weird or delightfully caricatured faces appear in wooden *Gigaku* masks (see Plates 233, 234). *Gigaku*, ritual dramas, seem to have been performed in temple courts only during the Nara period.

Yakushiji, another wonderful temple outside Nara, is important especially because of its magnificent sculpture and its unusual double-roofed pagoda (Plate 235). Buddhist art reached maturity with such superb figures as the Gakkō Bosatsu (Plate 236), and the Yakushi Buddha of Yakushiji, shown in Plate 237. The Bosatsu, originally gilt but now black with age, stands just over six feet high and is a masterpiece of the naturalistic, fully developed three-dimensional sculptural style that, while stemming from Chinese originals, is uniquely Japanese. The Yakushi Buddha, even more breathtaking, has the gentle expression and beautiful hands that reflect the religious idealism of this age.

228. The Hokke-dō of Tōdaiji, Nara (eighth century).

229. Figure of Fūkukenjaku Kwannon, dry lacquer (747).

230. Rushana Butsu, hollow-lacquer figure (759).

231. Kongō Rikishi, guardian figure (eighth century).

232. Meikira Taisho, clay guardian figure (mid-eighth century).

233. *Gigaku* mask in wood (eighth century).

235. The pagoda, Yakushiji near Nara (eighth century).

234. *Gigaku* mask in wood (eighth century).

236. Gakkō Bosatsu, gilt sculpture (*c.* 710).

237. Figure of Yakushi Buddha (*c.* 710).

238. Figure of Ashura, guardian of the Sākyāmuni Buddha, dry lacquer (Late Nara, eighth century).

239. Bust of Gobujo, dry lacquer (Late Nara, eighth century).

240. Figure of Furuna (dated 734).

The strangely Indian quality of a dry-lacquer figure of Ashura (Plate 238) is probably due to the fact that at this time, especially at Nara, foreign craftsmen working with the Japanese introduced styles from abroad. One of the only demon guardians who overcomes the enemies of Buddhism not only by strength but also by charm, Ashura is one of a series of eight figures authorized by the *Lotus Sutra* (one of the fundamental texts of Mahayana Buddhism) to be placed protectively around the Sākyāmuni Buddha. Gobujo (Plate 239) is also included in this supernatural group. Apart from these guardians ranged around the enthroned Buddha in the west Kondō hall of Kōfukuji, now destroyed, there were also figures of ten chief disciples, each endowed with a special power. Furuna, (Plate 240), for instance, who is one of them, had been granted the gift of eloquence in teaching the law, that is, the Buddhist doctrine.

During the eighth century, the capital was abruptly moved from Nara to Nagaoka.

The most likely reason for this was to reduce drastically the powers of the Buddhist clergy. Priests and monasteries could not be taxed; indeed they had to be supported, and the financial demands of the Nara clergy became more than the country could bear. Japan was not a rich land, and the move meant additional hardships. It is said that ten years of hard work by 300,000 laborers and one year's entire taxes were spent on Nagaoka. In 794, the new and still unfinished city was deserted, and for some mysterious reason the capital was moved again, this time to Heian, the "Capital of Peace and Tranquility" (modern Kyōto). The Heian period which followed was to last until 1185.

During the Heian period the real power of government began to pass to members of the Fujiwara clan, who by careful marriages into the imperial family opened the way to feudalism. The religious picture was transformed and stimulated by the introduction of two new sects: the Tendai, by Dengyō Daishi in 788, and the Shingon ("True Word"), by Kobo Daishi in 823. They taught not only meditative practices but also very complicated rituals including magic spells, symbols, and incantations. Long training and deep concentration was necessary to learn them, and it was perhaps because of this that these particular sects appealed especially to the sophisticated aristocracy. The largest Tendai and Shingon temples are generally found in isolated places, like Mount Koyo-san, free from worldly distractions. This new need for a different type of location brought about a revolution in the planning of monasteries.

Japan at this point departs rather sharply in her architecture from the Chinese schemes on which she has so far depended. No longer formally grouped around a courtyard, the buildings are scattered on a hillside, around a lake, or simply wherever the ground permits. Although they are not found in typically isolated spots, two good examples of the solid buildings of the early Heian period are the Pagoda of Daigoji in Kyōto, originally built in 951 and recently restored, and the Pagoda at Muroji near Nara (Plates 241, 242). The eaves are held up by triple, instead of the earlier double, supporting brackets, and the tones of the tinkling bronze bells on the pinnacles each symbolize a particular prayer. In the later Heian, or Fujiwara, period, there followed a noticeable lightening of architectural forms and an almost frivolous handling of detail. One of the most delightful Fujiwara buildings is the Hōōdo ("Phoenix Hall") of Byōdōin at Uji (Plate 243), which was dedicated to Amida, whose cult became popular at this time. The open colonnades leading inward to the hall create an air of enchantment; the main figure and the wood sculptures around the inner walls are the work of sculptor Jocho. A detail from one of the painted wooden doors, depicting Amida descending amid musicians, dancers, and worshippers, is seen in Plate 244.

Japanese sculpture gradually broke away from binding Chinese traditions during the Heian period, although in this era's earliest phases Chinese sculpture was still being imported. Early Heian sculpture generally projected a somber, bulky massiveness, like that of the ninth century Yakushi Nyorai, Buddha of Healing (Plate 245), and of the Empress Jingo (Plate 246), deified as the Shinto goddess Jingo-Kogo (although in her case the figure is only about twelve inches tall). The nearly life-size Yakushi Nyorai in Plate 245 and the Shaka Nyorai in Plate 247 are also typical of the period in that, with the exception of the set-in hands, they are carved from single blocks of wood (as is the Shinto deity holding a cermonial scepter in Plate 248). Wood, sometimes

242. The Pagoda at Muroji, near Nara (Heian).

241. The Pagoda of Daigoji, Kyōto (originally built in 951).

243. Hōōdo, or "Phoenix Hall," of Byōdōin at Uji (1053).

245. Yakushi Nyorai, wood sculpture (early ninth century).

247. Shaka Nyorai, wood sculpture (ninth century).

246. Carved figure of the Empress Jingo, painted wood (c. 890).

244. Detail of wooden door in the Phoenix Hall, by Jocho (Heian).

combined with lacquer, had become Japan's chief sculptural material; native sculptors would maintain this preference throughout their cultural history. An interesting example of wood and lacquer is the sensitively carved portrait of the monk Geien Sojo in Plate 249; lacquer, thinly applied to the face and body, has also been used as a binding for the sawdust layers which build up the

248. Carved Shinto deity, wood (Early Heian).

250. Divine warrior, wooden figure (late ninth century).

249. The monk Geien Sojo, carved wood with lacquer coating (early ninth century).

folds of the robe. We will constantly notice the Japanese preoccupation with facial characteristics and expressions, whether sublimely subtle or arrestingly exaggerated. The ferocity that is so often seen in the late Nara guardian figures seems to have lost its power in Heian sculpture; a ninth century divine warrior (Plate 250), once elaborately gilded and painted, looks more like a stylized dancer than a terrifying ogre.

At the beginning of the tenth century, China fell into confusion with the collapse of the T'ang dynasty. Direct contact with Japan was broken. But before the breakdown was complete, elements of new religious movements were accepted in Japan. Worship of Buddha Amida, the Redeemer, and Buddha of Boundless Light, quickly overshadowed other cults. The Fujiwara family grew more and more powerful. They built temples and gave protection and patronage to artists and craftsmen, among them Jocho, the master sculptor of the age. It was he who set a new standard for sculpture and who directed an important school in the eleventh century. His art strikes a balance between the humanity of the late Nara and the cool, monumental quality of the early Heian style. His wonderful Amida Nyorai (Plate 251), nine feet, eight inches in height, shows the gentleness Jocho brought to sculpture. Significant features of the new style of this period can be seen in the wooden figure in Plate 252: the downward-looking and barely opened eyes, which have the effect of drawing the viewer in toward the Buddha, the much wider lap, and a slightly more marked waistline. Another notable change in Fujiwara wood carving was the assembling of a large number of small wooden pieces so as to take visual advantage of the natural grains. This also made more delicate carving of detail possible, as may be seen in the hands of

251. Amida Nyorai, carving in wood, by Jocho (1053).

a statue of Yakushi Nyorai (Plate 253). This delicate treatment of hands and robes is displayed again in an interesting conceptualization of the much-admired historical figure, Prince Shōtoku Taishi. In a small shrine in the Hall of Painting, which is dedicated to the prince, he is represented as a precociously pensive boy of seven (Plate 254).

Generally speaking, all the arts flourished during the Heian period, particularly under the influence of Shingon. However, sculpture could not always cope with the demands of the complicated new sets of symbols and rituals. To fill the gap, painting, by necessity, developed very rapidly. Two basic

252. Figure of the Buddha, wood (eleventh century).

254. Prince Shōtoku Taishi as a boy of seven, wood sculpture by Enkai, painted by Hata Chitei (*c.* 1069).

253. Statue of Yakushi Nyorai, wood (1047).

types of picture emerged; both were in full color on silk and were kept rolled up as scrolls when not in ceremonial use, and both were based on ninth century Chinese models. One type, the Mandara, an exquisitely colored symbolic diagram used for contemplating the mysteries of Buddhist theology, gives the artist little opportunity to display originality of talent; the second type, a straightforward presentation of Buddhas, bodhisattvas, or religious narrative, allows somewhat more freedom and inventiveness. Four beautiful examples of this second type are seen in Plates 255 through 258. The bodhisattva Kokuzo (Plate 255), a guardian of compassion and possessor of all virtues, and the bodhisattva Fugen (Plate 256), who represents constancy in contemplation, are painted in the traditional poses already familiar in sculpture. The extraordinary refinement of these paintings is largely due to the brilliance of the colors, which now are somewhat mellowed with age, and also to such qualities as the discreet use of gold and silver, the fragile ornamentation, and the delicacy of the drawing. *Zenzai's Pilgrimage to the Fifty-five Saints* (Plate 257), with its stylized trees and water and deliberately distorted architecture, shows an early and more truly Japanese style that is in sharp contrast to the disciplined "Chinese style" of religious painting. A painting such as *One of the Sixteen Arhats* in Plate 258 (an arhat being one of the enlightened, saintly men of Hinayana Buddhism) falls somewhere between the two, but has none of the spontaneity or vivid charm associated with the most exciting new development in Japanese secular art—narrative painting.

Court life during the Fujiwara period reached unbelievable peaks of studied sensitivity, romanticism, and social and amorous gossip, and it was said that while the men

256. *Bodhisattva Fugen,* color on silk (Fujiwara).

257. *Zenzai's Pilgrimage to the Fifty-five Saints,* color on silk (Early Heian).

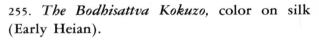

255. *The Bodhisattva Kokuzo,* color on silk (Early Heian).

258. *One of the Sixteen Arhats,* color on silk (Early Kamakura).

259. Detail from *Tale of Genji,* narrative scroll, ink and color on paper (Kamakura).

260. Detail from the *Matsuzaki Tenji-engi,* narrative scroll, ink and color on paper (fourteenth century).

gravely wrote bad Chinese, the women were content to write good Japanese. The most famous writer of the period was Lady Murasaki, who, considering herself an old woman at the age of thirty, wrote the world-famous *Tale of Genji.* This, along with other novels and legends, provided the inspiration for a unique form of expression, narrative painting. These often immensely long scrolls show a native tradition in draw-ing almost untouched by Chinese influence. The easy flow of line, the swift sense of movement, the subtle suggestion of space, and the remarkable freshness are all features that become dominant in this and the fol-lowing period (see Plate 259). This colorful style is called *Yamato-e* ("Japanese style"), as opposed to *Kara-e,* which is the Chinese.

During the twelfth century, both the Fujiwara family and the imperial house went into a decline. The elegance and refinement of the lives led by the pleasure-seeking and increasingly effeminate nobility were too far removed from reality to survive the military ambitions of local chieftains. The ultimate battle for power was waged by the ruthless Taira and Minamoto clans, both blood relations of the imperial house. Finally, in 1185 Minamoto Yoritomo succeeded in establishing himself as head of a military dictatorship at Kamakura. The age of the Shōguns, military governors, began when the powerful military class took actual charge of the government. Although the government moved to Kamakura, Kyōto remained the center of artistic life. It is probably for this reason that the changes in the arts of the period are not immediately apparent. Nevertheless, as one might expect, there appeared a greater vigor and severity as much of the Fujiwara elegance was stripped away in the face of a military dictatorship.

In spite of all this, the changes that occurred were only partly due to the new political regime. Contact with China was renewed, and the realism and insight of Ch'an (Zen) Buddhism and philosophy were introduced to Japan. Zen rejected with loathing the decadent worship of images and relics; instead, it searched for enlightenment and spiritual harmony in both disciplined meditation and the everyday aspects of life. Zen was to penetrate deeply into Japanese culture, bringing energetic rhythms to paintings, severity to architecture, and a new realism and power to sculpture.

The most interesting, important, and highly developed Japanese painting occurred during the Kamakura period—the narrative scroll paintings of the twelfth and thirteenth centuries appeared, in which the natural talent of the Japanese artist found its fullest expression. Vivid, realistic prose demanded illustrations as visually exciting and expres-

261. Detail from the *Life of Ippen*, narrative scroll, painted on silk (1299).

sive as the text. The compelling enthusiasm of the new masters of ink and color resulted in narrative paintings as varied in style as they were rich in color and unified in composition. The spectator is carried swiftly through one event to the next with the same sense of anticipation one feels when caught up in a fast-paced novel. This does not mean that detail is neglected. Depiction of amazement, sympathy, savage realism, humor, pathos, and caricature is to be found in small details, such as appear in the scenes from the *Matsuzaki Tenji-engi* (Plate 260) and from the *Life of Ippen* (Plate 261). This last is unique in that it is the only such illustration painted on silk.

The tendency toward detailed realism began to show itself in portrait painting, and is seen early in the Kamakura period in the portraits belonging to the Jingoji Monastery. With the exception of one, they are all painted in the usual Buddhist manner; but the one exception was to set a pattern for later ages. This particular painting (Plate 262) is interesting from a historical as well as an artistic point of view, as it presents a realistic likeness of Minamoto Yoritomo, founder of the Kamakura government. The angular outline and the simple coloring are basically similar to the treatment we see in the illustration for the *Tale of Genji* in Plate 259. The portrait of Minamoto Yoritomo was painted by Fujiwara Takenobu (1142–1205), who was the first in a long line of portrait painters. To say that his son, Fujiwara Nobuzane (1176–1268), followed in his footsteps becomes an understatement when we examine his *Portrait of Minamoto Kintada* (Plate 263). He far surpassed his father in simplicity of design and depth of character study.

Up to this time landscape painting had remained essentially a background feature in Japanese art, and it was not considered to be of fundamental importance until an interesting development occurred in connection with Dual Shinto (an art category wherein Shinto and Buddhist deities appear alongside each other). Shinto is a native religion of Japan; it is based on nature worship. It was in Dual Shinto-inspired painting that landscape began to emerge as a subject in its own right. In *Kasuga Mandara* (*c.* 1300) the deities, painted on silk, still manage to dominate the composition (Plate 264). But in an early fourteenth century painting inspired by Dual Shinto, *The Waterfall at Nachi* (Plate 265), only a small shrine, hidden almost entirely by trees, and the disk of the setting sun (hinting at the mystic union of the Buddha of Boundless Light and the Shinto "Great Sun of Truth") indicate any religious intention.

During the Heian period the guardians of the Buddha and the faithful were given a new importance in Japanese religious art, and gradually individual cults arose as each attracted his own following. Mahatejas, for instance, had the power to overwhelm the evildoer and protect the good. He could be invoked by spells, symbols, and magic words connected with his name and title. A Kamakura painting of him in lurid colors on silk (Plate 266) shows him at his most awe-inspiring.

An unlikely little fashion of the Kamakura period was the adornment of copies of the Buddhist scriptures, or sutras, with decorative paintings having absolutely no association with the text; according to Buddhist practice, this was supposed to be a means for the donor to acquire merit. Sometimes the paper was shaded with squares of gold leaf and scattered with gold

262. *Portrait of Minamoto Yoritomo,* color on silk, by Fujiwara Takenobu (twelfth to thirteenth centuries).

263. *Portrait of Minamoto Kintada,* ink and color on paper, by Fujiwara Nobuzane (Kamakura).

265. *The Waterfall at Nachi,* painting (early fourteenth century).

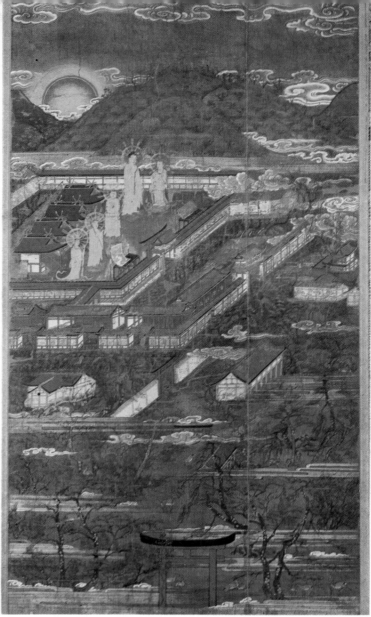

264. *Kasuga Mandara,* color on silk (*c.* 1300).

dust; the practice was carried to extremes, however, when an extract from one of the sacred scriptures was printed over a fan-shaped painting (Plate 267). A welcome somber contrast is the lightly colored portrait of Myōe Shōnin (Plate 268), a famous Zen Buddhist hermit, shown meditating serenely in a tree.

The most important sculptural work of the Kamakura period is either by Unkei or by members of his school. Unkei was born at Nara, where he was given the opportunity of studying the masterpieces of the region. He reinterpreted the humanist traditions of the great Nara era in the

266. *Mahatejas,* hanging picture, full color on silk (Kamakura).

267. *Sutra,* fan-face painting, ink and color on paper (Kamakura).

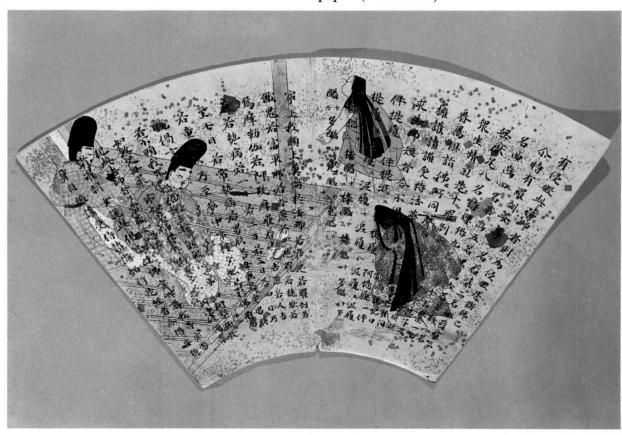

268. *Portrait of Myōe Shōnin,* ink and color on paper, attributed to Jonin (thirteenth century).

269. Memorial statue of Mūchaku, by Unkei (*c.* 1208).

realistic manner of the Kamakura period, his most interesting contribution being in the field of portraiture. Because painters and sculptors worked in schools and did not overly emphasize individual effort, Unkei's personal achievements are not easily identifiable. However, his statue of Mūchaku (Plate 269) shows the bold directness of his style as well as his keenly sensitive understanding of personality. Mūchaku was an Indian monk who had died a long time before this statue was made. It was just as natural for Unkei to use a Japanese model for this memorial statue as it was for the early Italian painters to use Italian women as models for the Virgin Mary. In any case, he has created a man instilled with the gentle compassion and understanding of one who has reached emotional and spiritual maturity.

Unkei's most astonishingly realistic innovation was the use of crystal for the eyes of his subjects. A wooden statue of an emaciated old man (Plate 270), one of the twenty-eight guardians of Senju Kwannon, borrows this trick later on. Another ingenious and charming concept of the early thirteenth century is to be seen in a statue by Kōshō of the priest Kuya (Plate 271); the tiny figures filing out of his mouth and into the air represent the pious words that he spoke in the name of Amida.

271. The Priest Kuya Preaching, figure by Kōshō (early thirteenth century).

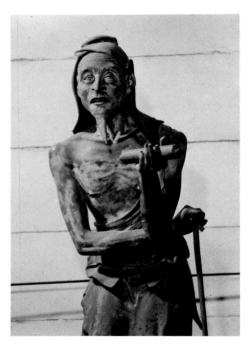

270. Wooden statue of Basu Senin, School of Tankei (1254).

Both Unkei's father, Kokei, and his disciple, Jōkei, were sculptors. Jōkei was extremely versatile; witness his painted wooden figure of Sho Kwannon, the goddess of mercy (Plate 272), the aggressively protective statue of the guardian Kongō Rikishi

272. Figure of Sho Kwannon, painted wood, by Jōkei (1226).

274. Figure of Vimalakīrti, in wood, by Jōkei (late twelfth century).

275. Wooden figure of Genko, attributed to Kokei (Kamakura).

273. Figure of Kongō Rikishi, in wood, by Jōkei (Kamakura).

(Plate 273), and the pathetically subdued figure of the ailing monk Vimalakīrti (Plate 274). Unkei's father, to whom the moving figure of a kneeling monk in Plate 275 has been attributed, also brought great strength to this new realistic style; Unkei's son, Koben, was responsible for the powerfully muscled demon lantern bearer, one of a pair, which appears in Plate 276.

Realism combined with hero worship reaches a peak in a magnificent thirteenth century portrait of a nobleman in the train of Prince Munekata (Plate 277). If at first glance his costume appears to be strangely clownish, we have only to observe his wearily haughty expression and the manner in which his right hand is held to know that we are in the presence of nobility and power.

The most famous relic of Chinese architectural style in the city of Kamakura is the Shariden, or Relic Hall (Plate 278). The

277. *Portrait of Uesug Shigefusa,* lacquered and painted wood (thirteenth century).

278. The Shariden, or Relic Hall (Kamakura).

276. Wooden figure of Tentoki, the demon lantern bearer, by Koben (1215).

main structure is raised up on a stone platform; the double roof, which would originally have been tiled, was thatched so as to make it easier to keep in good repair.

The authority of the Kamakura Shōguns gradually diminished, and they lost power completely in 1334, when one of their own, General Ashikaga Takauji, treacherously shifted his alliance to Emperor Go-Daigo, following the latter's daring escape from exile. Chaos was the eventual result, and Japan entered the long, confused period of civil war called the *Namboku-cho,* the "Northern and Southern Courts." Finally, in 1398, a faction headed by Ashikaga Yoshimitsu gained power, and an uneasy peace ensued. But the Ashikaga Shōguns of Kyōto never were able to subdue the rebellious minority, and consequently all the evils that accompany political weakness were felt throughout the next two centuries. Yoshimitsu's palace in the Muromachi section of Kyōto gave this period its name. Japanese civilization in the Muromachi period is marked by the spread of Zen Buddhism, the rise of ink painting, the pursuit of luxury, and the introduction of the tea ceremony.

The members of the court at this time were much more seriously bent on seeking pleasure than political stability, and in order to satisfy their expensive tastes they had to find new sources of income. Increasing trade with China supplied a solution to the problem, at least for the time being. Monks and "Official Embassies," which were usually composed of scoundrels, took an active part in shady international commercial ventures. These not only proved to be highly profitable, but helped to cause quite a transformation in the arts. To a considerable extent, the sudden shift in artistic trends may be attributed to the introduction of prized early Chinese paintings of the Sung and Yüan dynasties and to the increasingly rapid spread of Zen Buddhism. Zen's dismissal of scholarship and fussy ceremonies as well as its emphasis on simple living made it particularly attractive to those of the samurai, or warrior class, who cared nothing for learning and had, by necessity, already adjusted themselves to the frugal life.

As previously pointed out, Japanese painting of the preceding centuries fell into two categories: religious pictures such as the Mandaras, religious portraits or narratives; and secular art, such as narrative scrolls and portraits. With a few exceptions, the artists in both styles of painting, which had been created for temples or the refined tastes of the nobility, remained anonymous. With the Muromachi period, the situation changed; painting became more personal as artists began to sign their works. Art itself began to break free from courtly patronage, from religion, and from literature. One of the most beautiful examples of Zen art is the *Heron* (Plate 279), painted in the late fifteenth century by a brilliant artist named

279. *Heron,* painting by Tan-an (late fifteenth century).

Tan-an, who mysteriously disappeared while still a young man. This painting shows once and for all with what economy and deceptive ease a fine artist can express the true nature of his subject.

The most important feature of Far Eastern painting, as we have seen, is its emphasis on linear composition; this means that a picture relies for its effect on the pattern of its lines rather than on masses of color and subtlety of tone. However, subtlety of tone, as well as linear composition, plays an important part in the *suiboku* style, which literally means "black painting"; here the outlines become much stronger than in previous Japanese paintings, and they vary individually according to the speed and pressure with which the brush is applied. The subject matter of Japanese pictures also changes with the introduction of this mainly Southern Sung tradition, and landscapes are idealized to reflect the vitality of the natural world.

This style was at its peak during the lifetimes of such masters as Shūbun and Sesshū. Shūbun, a Zen Buddhist monk, was greatly influenced by Hsia Kuei and Ma Yüan, the two greatest landscapists of the Southern Sung dynasty. The way in which a gnarled pine reaches out into a misty void in Shūbun's *Landscape* (Plate 280) is reminiscent of Ma Yüan's style. *Winter Landscape* (Plate 281) is one of a pair of hanging scrolls by Sesshū (most probably a student of Shūbun's), an artist who gained firsthand knowledge of Sung art by traveling to China around 1468 and visiting well-known Ch'an (Zen) monasteries. An intensely powerful landscape by Kei Shōki, another Zen monk and follower of the Shūbun tradition, is seen in Plate 282. "Axe stroke" brushwork gives a sense of mass to the rocks, as we have seen earlier in Chinese painting, and the clarity of the little figures in the foreground is coun-

terbalanced by the hazy middle distance.

Alongside this highly developed style a new and colorful "genre" art sprang from the *Yamato-e* tradition. The earliest example of this (from the mid-sixteenth century) is a six-fold screen by Kano Hideyori entitled *Under the Maples at Takao*. A detail (Plate 283) shows a cheerful everyday scene of mothers and children enjoying the open air. The usual theme of contemporary genre painting was the four seasons, with each screen depicting two of the seasons.

The architecture of the Muromachi period was influenced by Chinese taste yet based, to

280. *Landscape,* ink painting, by Shūbun (early fifteenth century).

some extent, on traditionally simple Japanese forms. The main problem facing architects was how to meld these two conflicting elements without one's disrupting the other. The Ashikaga Shōguns were heavily dependent on the Zen monks, whose close links to China had been further strengthened by the increase in trade; therefore we encounter Chinese-influenced metropolitan monasteries like Tōfukuji (Plate 284). In secular buildings (Plates 285, 286) like the Golden and the Silver Pavilions (the former was burned down by a madman in 1950), the lightness of the main structure, the arched window openings, and the pine-shingle roofs are in the Japanese tradition.

A most important advance in this period is the inspired use of natural scenery, which designers made still more beautiful by perfectly chosen building sites and the creation of wonderful gardens. The austere influence of Zen can be seen in some, such as the sand garden of Ryoanji (Plate 287), where the five groups of rocks rising from the meticulously raked sand represent land masses in the midst of an ocean. Very different from this is the garden of Daisenin (Plate 288), representing a landscape in miniature: The camellia bushes in the background are meant to be clouds drifting round rocky mountain peaks, the sand a tempestuous river, and the mossy bank on the right a grassy hillside.

The cult of drinking tea originated in China among the followers of Zen. It was said by the monks to induce purity, tranquility, harmony, and reverence—all commendable, priestly qualities. Under the guidance of the tea master Sen-no-Rikyū, who was well versed in the art, tea drinking was established as a ceremony in Japan in the sixteenth century, and its effect on architecture was immediately visible. The teahouse (*chashitsu*) with its alcove (*tokonoma*),

281. *Winter Landscape,* hanging scroll, ink and light color, by Sesshū (fifteenth century).

in which were usually found a painting and a flower arrangement, mushroomed everywhere and single-handedly reduced architecture and decoration to their simplest,

282. *Landscape,* ink and color on paper, by Kei Shōki (fifteenth century).

most restrained forms. The tearoom, where only intellectual or artistic conversation was tolerated, was usually about nine feet square and could be entered only by crawling through a small opening. In the garden there would be a small trough with a dripping pipe above it so that guests might rinse their mouths and wash their hands before the ceremony. An iron teakettle of the Muromachi period and a deliberately uneven

ceremonial teabowl are seen in Plates 289 and 290.

During the last years of the Muromachi period Japan was once more devastated by a civil war. The country was divided up into numerous small feudal states, each under its own *daimyo,* or lord. Ultimately reunification under a strong central government was achieved by three great soldiers:

283. *Under the Maples at Takao,* detail from a six-fold screen, color on paper, by Kano Hideyori (mid-sixteenth century).

284. The main gate of Tōfukuji, Kyōto (Muromachi).

285. The Golden Pavilion of Rokuonji, on the outskirts of Kyōto (Muromachi).

286. The Silver Pavilion of Jishoji, on the outskirts of Kyōto (Muromachi).

287. The sand garden of Ryoanji, Kyōto.

288. The garden of Daisenin, Kyōto.

289. Iron teakettle (Muromachi).

290. Ceremonial teabowl (Muromachi)

Nobunaga, who was soon assassinated; Hideyoshi; and Tokugawa Ieyasu. This brief but stormy era, known as the Momoyama period, lasted from 1573 until 1615; it is of great importance both historically and artistically, as it was in these years that the foundations of the modern Japanese state were laid and new attitudes toward all the arts came to the fore. The new rulers were ambition-driven warriors of little or no learning who cared nothing for tranquil art; instead they demanded that everything be on a grand scale so that their new wealth could be suitably admired. Huge castles and many-storied mansions were erected, and it is not without reason that the period has been called the "Age of the Great Decorators." The Nishi Hoganji temple of Kyōto, with its relative complexity of design, is an example of the architecture of the short-lived Momoyama period. The exterior (Plate 291) suggests little of the ostentatious splendor lying within, such as the heavy gilt bird-strewn ceiling (Plate 292).

With the new tastes a brighter and more massive style of decoration was needed,

291. The Hiun-kaku of Nishi Hoganji, Kyōto (Momoyama).

292. The ceiling of the Shoin Hall in Nishi Hoganji, Kyōto (Momoyama).

especially for the sliding screens that were often used to partition a room. This need rapidly gave rise to a vigorous style of painting that was impressive if only for its very boldness of composition and color. Its effect was considerably heightened, furthermore, by a spendthrift use of gold. The great founders and masters of this style were the members of the Kanō family. They decorated vast numbers of screens and doors in this splendidly extravagant manner. Typical characteristics of the Kanō school are the bold large-scale composition, the firm outlines, and the heavy gilt background of the six-fold screen *Cedars and Pines in Snow* (Plate 293).

The older *suiboku* tradition would not be put aside by the brash new style, however, and was now inspired by the great Ch'an masters Liang K'ai and Mu Ch'i, of the Southern Sung period; Tohaku and Togan were its talented Japanese representatives at

this time, and they stood in direct opposition to the Kanō school. A mere glance at Tohaku's superb work will convince one of its overwhelming superiority. His exquisite composition of pine trees, grass, and flowers, shown in Plate 294, is a panel from a pair of screens painted in ink and full color on paper with a background of gold. Tohaku's handling of ink was unsurpassed in his own lifetime, and in the *suiboku* detail from a pair of screens executed in ink on silk (Plate 295), with its subtly balanced and contrasting relationship of tones, we see screen painting at its finest.

The final destruction of the house of Hideyoshi came with the fall of Osaka Castle in 1615. Tokugawa Ieyasu, however, had already moved the capital to Edo (modern Tokyo). In the ensuing Edo period (1615–1867) the rulers called for an isolated Japan. The country was virtually closed to foreigners with the exception of the Dutch

293. *Cedars and Pines in Snow,* **six-fold screen of Kanō school (Momoyama).**

294. Panel from a screen of pine trees, grass, and flowers; ink and color on paper, by Tohaku (Momoyama).

295. Detail of a screen painted in ink on silk, by Tohaku (sixteenth to seventeenth centuries).

296. *Hotei Fording a Stream*, ink painting, by Kanō Tanyū, Kanō school (nineteenth century).

at the city of Nagasaki, where they were confined until the Meiji restoration in 1868.

The economy was now based on money instead of rice as it had been for centuries. This change brought great hardship to the feudal lords, but gave the merchants the opportunity of making a fortune. Nevertheless, the Shōguns managed to keep up the feudal spirit by not allowing any excesses which might threaten their own authority; this resulted in a rigid class distinction, yet as long as the activities of each class did not infringe on the prestige of the military clans, they were able to develop in their own relatively free ways.

A new artistic situation arose owing to the fact that the tastes of each class had to be satisfied. The Kanō school, clinging to Momoyama tradition, worked almost exclusively for the Shōguns and produced a few talented artists like Kanō Tanyū before becoming so stuffily conservative that it lost all its strength and fell into disrepute. Tanyū possessed not only a masterful technique with brushes, but also an appealing sense of humor, as can be seen in *Hotei Fording a Stream* (Plate 296). During the nineteenth century European influence could be noticed in some Japanese art; the Kanō school, however, remained faithful to Chinese traditions of landscape painting. Many of their efforts, such as the *Landscape at Hagai* (Plate 297), are quite beautiful, though often lacking in vitality.

Korin was unquestionably the greatest master of the decorative school of painting that developed in Kyōto after the Momoyama period. There he became a court painter, and designed for both potters and lacquerers in the area, together with his brother Kenzan, who had considerable influence on ceramic design in the early years of the Edo period. *The Iris Screen* (Plate 298), probably the best known of Korin's works, is a brilliant display of his talent, in this case for creating a design using only blue, green, and gold on paper.

Aoki Mokubei (1763–1833), better known as a potter, was one of a number of gifted amateurs who made up a school known as the *Nanga* or *Bunjinga,* meaning "Southern Style" or "Literary Style," painters. They painted as a pastime and refused to follow any specific set of rules; the results could frequently prove as joyously graceful and gay as Aoki Mokubei's *Sunny Morning at Uji* (Plate 299).

The social and economic rise of the masses led to a rash of developments in the pictorial arts, especially in bustling Edo, where a new style of genre painting called *ukiyo-e,* the "floating world," appeared; unfortunately, the subject matter was usually limited to pictures of beautiful courtesans or actors, and the style was rather vulgar and shallow.

The introduction of printing in the early seventeenth century was of great importance. Hishikawa Morunobu (1618–1695) was the first artist to make use of this technique, later advanced by Suzuki Harunobu (1725–1770) and his followers. Harunobu was a very popular designer, with a special gift for depicting beautiful women and romantic scenes in prints (see Plate 300). A great artist of the theater was Toshusai Sharaku, a most remarkable print designer, whose career seems to have been squeezed into the one year of 1794, during which time he produced over one hundred dramatic head-

297. *Landscape at Hagai,* Kanō school, (nineteenth century).

and-shoulder portraits of famous Kabuki players (see Plate 301).

It was Katsushika Hokusai (1760–1849) who perfected the color print as a medium for landscapes, and in Plate 302 we see one of his collection *Thirty-six Views of Mount Fuji.* The spectacular effect is typical of his original and dramatic approach; in this picture the immense toppling wave takes on the terrifying aspects of a sea monster as the famous mountain rises sedately in the safety of the distance. Andō Hiroshige (1797–1858) was the second great landscape artist of the color print and produced many designs, including *Kambara* (Plate 303), from a series known as the *Fifty-three Stations on the Tokaido Highway.* He projected a gentle humor totally absent in the work of Hokusai and was particularly fond of rain and snow scenes.

Japanese art, which for the most part drew upon Chinese models, developed a distinct viewpoint of its own. It rejected some of the aloofness and sophistication of Chinese art and became more varied. It became, especially in more recent times, a vigorous art of the people.

299. *Sunny Morning at Uji,*
ink and color on paper,
by Aoki Mokubei (1824).

298. *The Iris Screen,* detail
of two panels, color
on paper, by Korin (Edo)

300. *Girls on a Verandah*, color print, by Suzuki Harunobu (*c.* 1766).

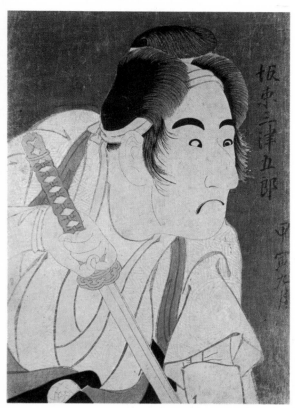

301. *The Actor Bando Mitsugoro in the Role of Ishi-i-genso,* color print by Toshusai Sharaku (1794).

303. *Kambara,* color print from the collection *Fifty-three Stations on the Tokaido Highway,* by Hiroshige (*c.* 1834).

302. Color print from the collection *Thirty-six Views of Mount Fuji,* by Katsushika Hokusai (1829 to 1831).

India

SHELTERED FROM the rest of the world by towering mountains and the sea, India has been blessed with both a geography and history that have fostered and stimulated a great tradition of national art. She has great size, an extensive variety of climate and of plant and animal life, and, most important of all, a human history of absorbing depth and complexity.

The size of India, roughly equal to Europe without Russia, has enabled her to take in a great range of different peoples, whose individual ways of life have been permitted to develop throughout an immense land. Yet her relatively compact land mass made possible an overall unity of a kind that China, as we have seen, found very difficult to maintain for any longer than the duration of a given dynasty.

India's climate must not be underestimated in its influence on her civilization; it varies from the fierce and devastating heat of the desert to the numbing chill of some of the world's highest mountains, and has created visual settings of vividness, grandeur, and excitement. The richness and variety of the animal and human life, set in the magnificence of these landscapes, has supplied an endless source of artistic inspiration.

We shall find that India's civilization is one of endless contrasts and contradictions between the natural and the idealized, between an earthy preoccupation with physical sensuousness and a cool mystical withdrawal from life, between coarse humor and a forbidding seriousness and exquisite serenity. Indian man is frequently at war not only with the elements but also within himself. For much of the year he is driven into a dreaming torpor by the inescapable heat,

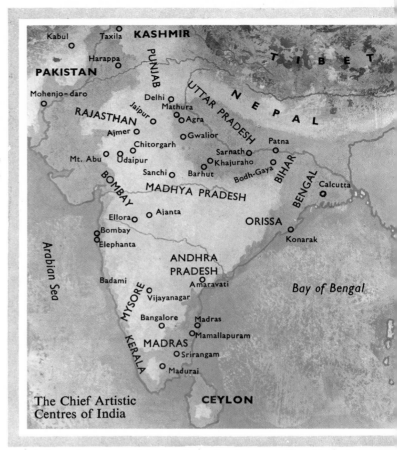

304. Map showing chief cultural centers of India.

INDIA FROM FIRST CIVILIZATION TO CLASSICAL AGE

Indus Civilization	*c.* 2500 B.C.–*c.* 1500 B.C.
Aryan invasion	*c.* 1500 B.C.
Ganges Civilization	*c.* 1500 B.C.–*c.* 400 B.C.
Rise of Buddhism and Jainism	before 500 B.C.
Maurya Empire and Successors	322 B.C.–A.D. 320
Mauryas	322 B.C.–185 B.C.
Shungas and Kanvas	185 B.C.–30 B.C.
Sātavāhanas	*c.* 50 B.C.–A.D. 250
Kushans: Gandhara and Mathura	*c.* A.D. 78–*c.* A.D. 250
Gupta Empire, Contemporaries and Successors	
Guptas	A.D. 320–600
Chalukyas of the Deccan	A.D. 550–642
Pallavas	A.D. 600–750
Harsha of Kanauj	*c.* A.D. 700

only to have his energies revived and his senses drastically quickened by the briskness of the winter and the monsoon. These extremes of climate intensify the contradictions in him, making him at once voluptuously sensual and spiritually chaste, a lover of raw life who is obsessed by an impulse to divorce himself from it and to deny utterly his natural physical reactions. It is precisely these various conflicts which have heightened the fascination and provocative uniqueness of Indian art.

Civilization came to India from the valley of the Tigris and Euphrates rivers, by way of ancient Persia. Although Indian civilization ranks as one of the oldest in history, this fact was not established until the English and American excavations during the third and fourth decades of this century. These led to the discovery of the Indus culture. In the third millennium B.C. the village communities in the mountains to the north of the Indus plain (see map on page 142, Plate 304) had reached a stage where they could receive and absorb Mesopotamian culture. Contacts with "the land between the rivers," and the mutual exchange of wares and ideas, consequently produced the Indus civilization.

This was the first major introduction of Mesopotamian and Persian culture into India. Unlike the peoples of the Tigris and Euphrates region, whose society was founded on a central authority, the peoples of India were not so unified; the Indus civilization was broken down into the fragmented pattern of separate villages living under no organized system of control. Only religion brought the separate villages together, to worship both the fertility of the soil (in the form of a mother goddess) and the cattle, which played an essential role in their primitive farming.

305. Statue in terra-cotta (Indus).

306. Statuette of a bull in terra-cotta (Indus).

307. Toy cart with oxen (Indus).

A small terra-cotta statue of the mother goddess appears in Plate 305. She wears a peculiar headdress, unknown outside India, with a fan-shaped top and two basketlike additions on either side of the head. The figure is soot-stained, indicating its probable use as a lamp. She is sparsely dressed, differing in this way from mother goddesses elsewhere, who are traditionally represented naked.

The statuette of a short-necked garlanded bull in Plate 306 and the toy cart with oxen in Plate 307 are very common in Indus art. The shape of the cart is virtually identical to that of those found in the area today.

With increasing trade, further settlements and outposts sprang up; it is thought that many of these were small commercial and industrial centers. Two main cities emerged—Mohenjōdaro and Harappa. They were equipped with avenues, palaces, brick and mud-plastered houses, bazaars, granaries, barracks for police or slaves, riverside quays and storage houses, and mighty citadels encircling temples and other religious buildings. These last had none of the imposing grandeur usually associated with a religious civilization. Art existed simply to serve ceremonial and practical ends.

New light has been thrown on one especially intriguing aspect of the Indus civilization as a result of the discovery of various carved soapstone seals such as the one shown in Plate 308. One of the most acceptable theories put forth by experts as to their purpose is that they were used primarily for trade and for the protection of goods or property. It seems that when merchandise was packed in bales, clay labels were affixed that bore the imprints of the seals; cotton fabric bearing an Indus Valley seal has been discovered at a prehistoric site in Iraq. They may also have been used as stoppers for vases. The seals most commonly show a bull-like animal with a single horn standing before a brazierlike artifact, the symbolism of which remains a mystery. An as yet indecipherable script always appears above the beast, which in less frequent instances may be an elephant, rhinoceros, crocodile, antelope, or such. Whereas the animal representations are extremely naturalistic, the rare attempts at human images on the seals are stiff and graceless. (See Plate 309.)

308. Steatite (soapstone) seal depicting figure of bull (Indus).

309. Steatite (soapstone) seal (Indus).

Indus sculpture is significant in that some of the figures in stone, bronze, and clay introduced distinctive artistic elements which were to become permanent characteristics of Indian art. One of the most vital of these is the rhythmic movements of the body, especially in the act of dancing. A copper statuette (Plate 310) prophetically hints at the classical Indian artist's single-minded obsession with the dance.

Terra-cotta was a favorite material with the Indus sculptors; the quality of their endeavors was not very distinguished—a fact which is borne out by the technically primitive, crudely modeled bust of a man in Plate 311. Of higher artistic value is the handsomely stylized steatite (soapstone) head in Plate 312, in which the hard masklike facial planes, the shape of the beard, which leaves a shaven upper lip, and the hair indicated by incised lines give positive evidence of Mesopotamian influence in the Indus valley.

It is not known exactly how and why the Indus civilization disastrously disintegrated, but by the middle of the second millennium B.C. a ruling class had evolved whose power was apparently shaken fatally. Citizens who had previously taken pride in their standard of living no longer continued to build new houses and, jammed in together, literally permitted the walls to fall down about them. They were ripe for conquest, which was to come at the hands of the Aryans. These seminomads from inner Asia probably possessed a knowledge of iron and a superior breed of horses, which must have made their victory all the more easy. In any case, the people of the Indus civiliza-

310. Statuette of dancing girl, copper (Indus).

began. The basic philosophies of the Indian religions—transmigration (samsara), the passage of a soul at death into another body; and nirvana, liberation from spiritual restlessness, pain, worry, and the outside world— were born. Vedic Brahmanism is the most ancient form of Hindu religion. Vedic mythology is not clear; no statues, paintings, or temples exist to tell us of the various gods; only the written hymns of the *Rig-Veda* give the slightest knowledge of the feats the deities performed. Even so, the characters of these gods are not sufficiently defined for us to distinguish one from another.

Little, if anything, of the art of the Ganges civilization remains, because perishable materials such as wood and earth were most commonly used. Fortunately, a gray terra-cotta statuette of the established mother goddess may be seen in Plate 313.

tion tried to crowd into those towns which were fortified in order to save themselves. Their end must have been a terrible one; skeletons have been discovered which indicate that many were massacred on the spot and left unburied.

After the first period of conflict, the Aryans adopted the Indians' way of life. However, whereas the Indus farmers had known only how to grow wheat, the Aryans had mastered the technique of rice growing. For this reason they moved from the fields of the Indus to the rice belt of the Ganges. There on the riverbanks a new way of life

311. Bust of a man in terra-cotta (Indus).

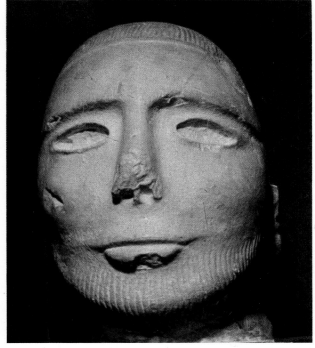

312. Head of a man in steatite (Indus).

313. Statuette of the mother goddess (Ganges civilization).

The figure is greatly exaggerated to emphasize feminine procreativeness and protrudes toward the front. It shows a technical advance over the Indus Valley statuettes in that the sculptor has separately molded the individual parts before assembling them.

The few writings of the period that have been found reveal a familiarity with iron, lead, tin, silver, and gold as well as with cotton, silk, and woolen garments, some of which were embroidered.

The Ganges valley, originally a dense and pathless forest, has been drastically changed by cultivation. However, certain isolated sites have revealed a number of copper axes, chisels, rings, harpoon heads and spearheads, swords, and strange anthropomorphic objects (things not human but which have been given human aspects) such as the mysterious artifact in Plate 314.

Architecturally this was a highly significant period, in which most types of Indian building emerged: the vihara, or monastery; the chaitya, or hall of worship; and the stupa, a royal or sacred burial mound. Village railings and gateways afterward became forms of great decorative importance. So, too, did the basically modest village hut with its bamboo beams, rectangular boxlike shape, and curved or bulbous top.

The next meaningful episode in the history of Indian art revolves about an empire set up by Candragupta Maurya after a Persian model. Under his grandson, the Emperor Aśoka, the Maurya state became the first and last Indian empire to encompass the entire subcontinent.

From the Maurya period (322–185 B.C.), and especially in the reign of Aśoka, there are to be found the first architectural and sculptural monuments in stone. Persian influence becomes quite obvious in the more than thirty monolithic columns (meaning they were made of a single piece of stone) which

Aśoka had dramatically erected around the country. Monumental animals topped their stylized lotus capitals (the uppermost sections of the columns). A magnificent example of one of these Mauryan works of art is the powerful, gleaming lion ringed with geese in Plate 315. The glistening surface sheen has never since been matched in Indian sculpture.

Following the brutal suppression of a provincial revolt, Aśoka suffered a grave spiritual crisis, which was to have a profound effect on Indian art. Appalled by the grisly experience, he became a fervent convert to the relatively young religion of Buddhism, with its burning concern for human welfare and justice. His monolithic columns bore

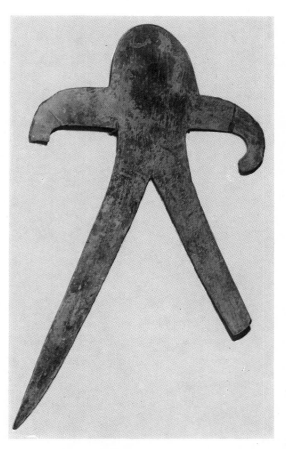

314. **Anthropomorphic figure (Ganges civilization).**

inscriptions of Buddhist law, as did many incised stones which were set about to influence the religious thought of his people. With the same crusading zeal, he set up countless stupas as shrines for holy relics. Stupas are without doubt the most important monument in the realm of Buddhist art. Their basic form may be seen in Plate 316. These two stupas are known as Stupa One and Stupa Three (Plate 316). They have three elementary parts: the dome resting on the base, the enclosed balconylike structure on top surmounted by umbrellas, and the railing, all of which are symbolic. The dome represents the "world mountain" or the "vault of the firmament"; the balcony enclosure is meant to be the little house of the gods who rule the earth, with the umbrellas symbolizing other heavens rising one above the other into infinity; and the railing represents the continuously revolving stars, hours, and seasons.

The most perfectly preserved Buddhist monument in India is the Great Stupa at

315. **Capital of an Aśokan column (Maurya period, third century B.C.).**

316. **View of Stupa One and Stupa Three at Sanchi (Shunga period).**

Sanchi (Stupa One). Built originally in brick by Aśoka, it was later enlarged to nearly twice its size. It was finally completed in the late first century B.C. Buddha was represented not by a statue but by such symbols as his footsteps, a lotus flower, a wheel, and a seat or bench under the Tree of Enlightenment. These symbols were depicted in relief together with less important divinities, nymphs, heavenly guardians, and mythical creatures adapted to Buddhist mythology from legendary stories, as well as elaborate motifs of flowers and vegetation. The fantastic gateways of the Great Stupa, guarded by the four lokapalas, familiar to us from Chinese Buddhist art, are astonishing in the richness and variety of their detail. The lokapalas were known to Indian Buddhists as the "four kings" of the four basic directions: Virudhaka, of the south, ruled the weird Kumbhandas, potbellied gnomes with stunted arms and legs who may be seen supporting the superstructure of the gate in Plate 317. Kuvera, sometimes called Vaisravana, ruled the north; his subjects were the yakshis and yakshas, genies of good or evil temperament, the most dangerous of whom were thought to seduce young men in order to devour them. A first-century bust of a yakshi heavily adorned with jewelry is seen in Plate 318. Dhritarashtra, guardian of the east, was the leader of the Gandharvas,

318. Bust of a yakshi, Bharhut (Shunga period, first century B.C.).

celestial musicians. Virupaksha, of the west, was king of the Nagas, some of the most intriguing figures in Indian mythology. Part serpent and part human, they were believed to live in treasure-laden palaces at the bottoms of lakes. As masters of the rains, they were extremely important in a country where water has always been a precious commodity; each possessed additional magic powers, owing to a fabulous jewel embedded in his head or throat. Buddha was said to have converted some of the

317. Detail of western gateway of Stupa One (Sātavāhana, first century B.C.).

Nagas; but none of these various creatures was considered immortal, and all had to endure transmigration as any mortal would.

A detail of a gateway at Stupa One is shown in Plate 319. It is the only one at Sanchi with the greater part of its ornamental figures intact. The reliefs are representative of Sātavāhana craftsmanship and are totally free from the stiffness of art of the Maurya period. The human faces have acquired expression, and their bodies have acquired natural movement and grace. All the reliefs are executed with the delicacy of ivory carvings; and the original religious intention aside, they convey a picture of contemporary manners, weapons, decorations, and symbolisms.

The vitality and the power of Indian sculpture are found at their greatest in the Deccan, the region where Karli is located.

In Plate 320, man, proud and self-assured, is shown together with woman, although each figure is complete in itself. They no longer appear entwined in decorative vegetation, an element which had been gradually restricted to incidental importance.

In the first century A.D. there were very important and interesting developments in Indian art. In the northwest the people had absorbed late Hellenistic or ancient Greek and provincial Roman culture through the borderland of Bactria, a geographic area which in modern times is known as Afghanistan and Turkistan. Before this, motifs and techniques had been borrowed by Indian artists and builders from Achaemenid Persia (such as the bell capital and monumental animals of Persepolis). Foreign influences had penetrated as far south as Amaravati, but the Indians lost no time in integrating

319. **Detail of the eastern gateway at Stupa One, Sanchi (Sātavāhana period).**

320. Relief from Karli (Sātavāhana period).

the new ideas, incorporating them so deftly into their own art that the final results appear to be essentially Indian; no matter how strikingly different the original ideas and forms, they inevitably emerged pulsing with life in the gracefully supple and sensitively expressive style of India.

During this first century A.D. a barbarian horde called the Kushans were violently driven south from their central Asian territories by other tribes. They established an empire in India. On the south, the new empire was bordered by Dravidian India. The Dravidians were the original inhabitants of India before the Arayans arrived. Within Dravidian India there were a great number of Indian languages, and on the north and east the country was bordered by central Asian tribes and by China. Within this realm, one region, Gandhara, and one city, Mathura, played a vital part in the history of Indian art. They became rival influences in the artistic melting pot of the powerful Kushan empire. Gandhara, made up of Pakistan and part of Afghanistan, embraced the westernmost part of north India, which had once fallen to Alexander. Mathura lay on the river Jumna, a hundred miles south of Delhi, at the center of the old Ganges civilization. It was for these historical and geographical reasons that the art of Mathura, with its strong national character, would eventually prevail over Gandhara's, with its tendency to follow imported traditions.

Set in a fertile plain, Mathura was at the center of a network of roads, with trade routes to Rome and the West. Nevertheless this ancient city was proudly conscious of its Aryan heritage. With the example of earlier Indian artists behind them, Mathura sculptors developed their own new approach to glorifying Buddha and his religion. The Buddhism of the Kushan dynasty was different from the Buddhism which had produced the stupas and sculpture of the Sanchi site.

The old school of belief, the Hinayana or "Lesser Vehicle," regarded the historical Buddha, Gautama, as a great teacher who had revealed the ways in which man could save himself from an endless cycle of rebirths. Gautama had preached the necessity of liberating oneself from all the worldly desires that bind the spirit to the ugliness of physical existence; at the same time he had been deeply concerned with freeing others from misery.

But in the time of the Kushan dynasty, the new school of thought called Mahayana, or "Great Vehicle," rapidly gained ground. Buddha was made more than human. Furthermore, a lesser group of divine beings, the compassionate bodhisattvas, was added to assist him in saving mankind. As we have mentioned earlier, the bodhisattvas selflessly put aside their own liberation and admittance to nirvana so that others might reach this ultimate goal.

For the first time, we begin to see the Buddha physically represented in sculpture. Gandhara sculptors draped their figures of Buddha and of bodhisattvas in a distinctly Greek manner (see Plate 322). It shows the Buddha in the "lotus posture" of meditation, and below the main figure is a relief of two Buddhas, each with a follower.

Narrative Buddhist sculpture of the Gandhara school is seen at its descriptive best in *The Temptation of the Buddha* in Plate 321. The Buddha was said to have received the "great enlightenment" while meditating under the bo tree. This work, based on that crucial event of his life, shows him seated under a bo tree while his tormentors, hordes of warriors and diabolical fiends, are viciously trying to distract him from the

321. *The Temptation of the Buddha* (Gandhara school).

322. *The Buddha in Meditation* (Gandhara school).

from the Valley of Swat shown in Plate 324. Notice how the umbrella-shaped canopies have become as broad as the stupa itself. The next step was to turn them into stories high above the stupa, which was divided into stories as well. Later still, the stories became uniform and rose in tiers, foreshadowing the curved-roof pagodas of Chinese and Japanese temples and monasteries.

The Kushans made Mathura their sum-

323. Buddhist reliquary from Bimaran, gold (Kushan period).

meditation which will lead to his enlightenment.

The earliest existing work of the Hellenized Gandhara school is a golden Buddhist reliquary (Plate 323), a receptacle for religious relics, in which the provincial Roman style can be noticed in the eagles with spread wings, and a general Western influence is apparent in the poses of the Buddhist figures.

Taxila, not far from the Gandhara region, was the site of a colossal 683-foot-high stupa erected by Kanishka, the greatest ruler of the Kushan dynasty. The Kushans had become Buddhists, but as usual their artists, who had inherited Greco-Roman traditions, insisted on handling old Indian architectural forms in their own way. Little of Kanishka's stupa remains, but it must have been very much like the beautiful little model

325. *The Visit of Indra to the Buddha* (Mathura school).

mer residence. Its workshops turned out a large supply of statues in red or pink sandstone, the mark of Mathura sculpture. The Mathura artists, as we shall see, tried to give their Buddha figures a feeling of touching human compassion and contemplative thought.

A relief entitled *The Visit of Indra to the Buddha* (Plate 325) has a softly rolling rhythmic vitality which is purely Indian. In this narrative frieze, Indra, king of the gods, humbly approaches the cave where Buddha awaits him. The attendant holds a fly whisk and is followed by Indra's elephant.

Other examples of Mathura sculpture range from frankly sensual studies of the female body (Plate 326) to a cruel and frighteningly expressive head with ram's horns (Plate 327).

Eighteen centuries of Aryan civilization, interrupted by invasions and the absorption of foreign cultures, now awaited a unifying force. That force appeared when the provincial Gupta dynasty, from the region of

324. **Small stupa from the Valley of Swat (Kushan period).**

326. *Woman under a Tree* (Mathura school).

327. Head with ram's horns, stone (Mathura school).

Bihar in the Ganges valley, conquered northern India as far as the Deccan. The Gupta empire thus established flourished in the fourth and fifth centuries A.D., and its rulers gave India the order and stability which were necessary for the rebirth of national literature and the arts. Sanskrit displaced the popular languages as the sole language of poetry and learning, and two major collections, the *Mahābhārata* and *Rāmāyana,* storehouses of Indian lore, were laboriously edited during this period. They recorded and enshrined all the various beliefs that Hinduism had accumulated since early Vedic times. The themes of the Hindu religion were vastly more fascinating and colorful than those of its younger relative, Buddhism, and offered an exciting and wholly new world of artists to explore. Happily, there were no ill feelings between Hindus and Buddhists in this civilized and sophisticated era. Influenced by these different trends, the culture of India blossomed under the Guptas, creating what was to remain a foundation of Indian life ever after. That beauty, good, and truth were one and the same was the belief which dominated art, manners, and in fact all of life in this splendid civilization.

In Gupta works of art Buddhist spirituality expresses itself with an extraordinary purity of line and in clear and harmonious shapes that, while being very much idealized, seem vibrantly alive. By the fifth century the Indian Buddha figure conveyed both the sublimely soulful quality of a great religious leader and the physical sensuousness so much a part of Indian art. Both qualities are portrayed by simplified facial planes and by a clinging drapery that revealed the body beneath it, as seen in Plates 328 through 330.

Hinduism, the oldest religion in India, developing from the old Brahmanism of Vedic times, again became popular, and

328. **Head of the Buddha from Mathura (Gupta period).**

Buddhism began to fade in India. As more people took up the old religion, Hinduism was faced with the problem of providing buildings for its worshippers. Unlike Buddhist worship, which is congregational, Hindu devotions can be performed before an image in private. The Hindu temple is the residence of the god and needs only a place for his image and a separate place of shelter for the worshipper. First the Hindus looked to earlier Buddhist buildings for a solution. The stupa inspired a round temple with shallow projections on four sides; the chaitya suggested a rectangular hall with a barrel-vaulted roof. But the final answer proved to be a flat-roofed square cella, an enclosed inner room housing the statue of a divinity, with a door on one side and a porch in front of it for the worshipper. This simple-sounding plan bears little resemblance, however, to the subsequent results. Story was piled upon story, the plain porch became an elaborate structure set about with impressive columns, and soon the overwhelming towers of Hindu temples loomed majestically up into the sky. Most of the larger monuments of the Guptas, including Narasimhagupta's three-hundred-foot-high temple at Nalanda, have disappeared. Narasimhagupta's monument would have been taller than any now exist-

329. **Statue of the Buddha from Nalanda (Gupta period).**

330. **Statue of the Buddha from Sarnath (Gupta period).**

ing. According to a contemporary Chinese traveler, it looked like the shrine at Buddh Gaya (Plate 331), which was completed during the Gupta period, in A.D. 526. There, on the site of the sacred bo tree under which Buddha received his enlightenment, stands another tree planted from a branch of the original. This and the temple of Mahabodhi are considered to be the center of the universe by Buddhist pilgrims. Owing to centuries of well-meant restorations, it would be impossible to state flatly that the temple looks precisely as it once did.

In India, dancing was a ritual in temples and festivals as well as a social accomplishment; its gestures and poses began to seep into Gupta sculpture. For all Gupta sculptors, Hindu or Buddhist, the human figure was the principal subject. Together with other artists they considered dynamic rhythm to be the most essential element of their works. Above all they cherished the idea of youth expressing itself with all its natural beauty and passion in rhythmic movement.

Frequently this enthusiasm inspired works full of movement, like the headless relief of Durga, the goddess destroyer of the buffalo demon (Plate 332).

332. Headless relief of Durga (Gupta period).

331. Temple of Mahabodhi at Buddh Gaya (Gupta period).

333. **General view of the caves of Ajanta (second century B.C. to seventh century A.D.).**

Somes of the most astounding and sublime works of Indian art are to be seen in the caves at Ajanta, Ellora, and Elephanta in the Deccan. This region actually lay outside the Gupta empire but had accepted and absorbed its artistic values and techniques. It was during the fifth century that Gupta influence first reached the Deccan. At Ajanta, religious cave sculpture and painting were carried on for almost eight hundred years. A general view of the complex of twenty-nine Buddhist caves near the source of the river Waghora is seen in Plate 333. They were accidentally discovered by some soldiers in 1819, and were at once acknowledged to be among the most spectacular creations of artistic genius and religious devotion in the world. Six of the cave temples were carved with magnificent relief sculpture by Hinayana Buddhists, and the rest by the later Mahayana sculptors of Gupta times. These reliefs illustrate the major Buddhist contribution to sculpture: their creation of perfectly balanced and weightless human figures in relief which

float in a world of their own, emerging magically from the deeply cut stone rather than being planted squarely on the ground.

Other wall spaces at Ajanta are covered with painted murals that glow with what we in the West have come to call "Indian splendor." Buddhist painters had developed their own formal principle of composition, known as "forthcoming." In "perspective," as we know it, objects become smaller and smaller as they finally disappear into the distance. In "forthcoming," the background is painted flatly so that the central figures, in contrast, can surge rhythmically forward and command the attention of the viewer. One can envision this as corresponding to a stage, where figures are seen in front of a backdrop.

Details of the superb façade of cave 19, a Mahayana chaitya, are shown in Plate 334. Hinayana symbols such as the Buddha wheel mingle freely with Mahayana figures, but plant design, as at Karli, is again restricted to the role of minor decoration. The Buddha wheel, which we have seen earlier in Buddhist

335. Cave 26 at Ajanta (Gupta period).

336. Colonnade of cave 2 at Ajanta.

334. Detail of the facade of Ajanta, cave 19 (Gupta period, first half of the sixth century A.D.).

art, was known as the "Wheel of the Doctrine" and symbolized, among other things, the cycle of birth and rebirth. Among the many intriguing motifs and figures are the miniature horseshoe windows with peeping heads shown in Plate 334. It seems incredible that all of this has been hand-carved out of a hillside of rock. Cave 26 (Plate 335) was finished during the Gupta period in the first half of the sixth century A.D. and is similar to cave 19 in its overall arrangement and architectural treatment. But the detail here is coarser and lacks 19's perfect balance. At the end of the hall we are met with a stupa within a chaitya, and it bears a beautifully chiseled figure of the Buddha.

Cave 2 follows the classic vihara pattern. The earliest viharas were plain halls with no columns. The first attempts at erecting pillars in these caves were not successful. Finally, architects came to the conclusion that the colonnade (a series of columns set at regular intervals) would work most effectively. These columns in cave 2 (Plate 336) were delicately cut with a jeweler's precision. Two giant seated divinities are to be found in the same cave. These massive figures nearly touch the ceiling and were once brightly painted. This type of imposing massiveness came to be an identifiable feature of the art of the Deccan. The paintings in cave 2 rank among the finest at Ajanta and, like all the others, were executed by large groups of artists. The elaborately designed ceiling, shown in Plate 337, gives an impression of great richness despite the limitations of its color; its design centers about a star-shaped white lotus, a common decorative motif.

Skill in painting as well as in dancing was considered a social grace by the Guptas. Courtesans, young women of unusual beauty and vague morals, were expected by their admirers to be adept artists. A portrait of

337. Ceiling of cave 2 at Ajanta.

338. Courtesan, detail of an external mural from cave 17 at Ajanta.

one of these enchantresses appears in a mural in cave 17 (Plate 338); slender, slit-eyed, and tastefully bejeweled, she suggests an extremely sophisticated way of life and the Gupta taste for material luxury. In contrast to those of earlier caves, the figures in cave 17's murals are smaller and crowd the compositions, giving them a busily narrative effect. A vivid example is the scene from *Vishvantara Jataka,* the story of Prince Vishvantara (Plate 339). Here, one is given absolutely none of the religious feeling of a Jataka (a story of a former life of the Buddha) as the eye is led in an almost nervous way from situation to situation and from figure to figure in the burning amber light. Nevertheless, Buddhas and bodhisattvas dominate the multitude of mythical, legendary, historical, and courtly figures seething across the walls at Ajanta. The air of luxury and ornate refinement leaves its mark on them, though, as suddenly Buddha, while maintaining an expression of spiritual preoccupation, appears as a prince

in dangling ornaments and black, tendril-like curls that probably have their origin in vine decorations (see Plate 340). This Jataka deals with his preaching among the women.

Female figures play an important role in the many palace scenes of Ajanta. Their small-waisted, voluptuous figures and softly rounded faces were frequently idealized to the point of making them look all alike.

The earliest indication of Indian skill in painting is a Mauryan period (beginning 321 B.C.) drawing of an elephant beside one of the Emperor Aśoka's religious stones. A very few Sātavāhana paintings have been preserved from pre-Gupta times, when the Ajanta caves held nothing more than one monastery consisting of two small chaityas; these Sātavāhana paintings illustrated Jataka stories in the naturalistic style of the Sanchi stupa reliefs. The only known Gandhara paintings, murals decorating a stupa at Miran, have reminded more than one Indian art historian of the wall paintings uncovered in Pompeii. The Guptas filled their houses

339. Mural from cave 17 at Ajanta (the story
of Prince Vishvantara).

340. *The Buddha Preaching among Women,* cave
1, Ajanta.

and monasteries with stylized paintings that emphasized the dance, and Buddhist priests made use of painted banners, conducting their preaching much in the manner of modern slide lectures, but the overall effect was one of artificialty. It is the masterful cave paintings which artistically soar above the rest.

After the Guptas, Hinduism triumphed over Buddhism and gradually assumed its place as the dominant religion of India. Hindu beliefs did not encourage large-scale wall painting, and consequently mural art declined. Sculpture, since it reflects light, was well suited to Hindu cave sanctuaries and the exteriors of their enormous temples. This form of Hindu art is seen at its best in the seventh- and eighth-century cave temples of Ellora in Hyderabad and in those of Elephanta near Bombay.

The sculpture of Ellora is the work of three religions, and was created over a period of nearly fifteen centuries. The Vishva-karma (Plate 341) is a Buddhist chaitya, and among the Hindu caves is the Rameshwaram (Plate 342). The decoration of the Hindu caves is simpler than that of the Buddhist caves, but they are often more elegant and generally honor the god Siva. The Vedic hymns taught that Siva was a good and generous god, but later Hinduism worshipped a trinity, the Trimurti, which was described this way: "The Absolute manifests himself in three persons—Brahma the Creator, Vishnu the Preserver, and Siva the Destroyer." In his different manifestations Siva could become Lord, the Great God; a teacher; Time, the destroyer of all things; and, among his other possible forms, the coolest and most detached or the most diabolically raging of the gods. He was known to wear necklaces of dead men's heads, bracelets of snakes, a crescent moon and a skull in his headdress. It was also

341.

342. Two caves from Ellora.

said that Siva smeared his body with cow-dung ashes and, at his worst, acted as chief of all the ghouls, vampires, hideous phantoms, and other obscene spirits that nightly lurked about in impure places. In yet another guise, he appears in a wall relief from the great cave at Elephanta as half man, half woman (Plate 343); to the left is the male half, which grasps a serpent, one of his symbols; on the right the female half holds a convex mirror.

During the sixth century the Hindu temples of Aihole and Vatapi (now Badami) were hewn out of rocky hillsides, and their walls, pillars, and ceilings carved with figures

344. *Vishnu Reclining on the Serpent Ananta* (Chalukyan period).

of Siva, Vishnu, and other Hindu divinities. The village of Aihole, about nine hundred miles from Bombay, was the capital of a large part of central and southern India ruled by the Chalukya dynasty from A.D. 550 to 642. Aihole stood between two traditions— the southern, with its sinuous grace, and the Deccan, with its power and stunning volume; the relief of Vishnu in temple 9 (numbers have been given them by scholars for easy identification) at Aihole is closely related to the first school (see Plate 344). The original name of the serpent upon which he is lying was Shesha; he was a Naga king who wished to win pardon for the sins of his race. Brahma agreed to this, saying, "Henceforth thou shalt live forever and shalt be called Ananta" ("eternal"). Ever since, Ananta has acted as support to the earth; Vishnu reclines upon him while sleeping, in order to bring forth a new world.

The artists during the Chalukya period interpreted and passed on the art of others; their major advance was in their refinement of techniques for the quarrying and tooling of great blocks of stone. The people of the

343. **Mural relief of Siva at Elephanta.**

345. Details and views of Mamallapuram (Pallava period).

347. Fountain figure (Pallava period).

346. Details and views of Mamallapuram (Pallava period).

Pallava kingdom were more creative and achieved the first southern culture independent of northern influence. The richest Pallava site is at the town of Mamallapuram, once the seat of royal power, at the rocky edge of the coast not far from the city of Madras. Here are to be found cave shrines, carved cliffs, a masonry temple, and five small monolithic temples fashioned from the huge granite boulders that litter the landscape. Superb monolithic elephants, lions, and oxen stand among those shrines as naturally as if they had wandered there from the jungle (see Plates 345 through 346). In Plate 347, we can see the Sanchi sculptors' sense of humor in the grotesque fountain figure.

After the Gupta empire came to an end, central and southern India gradually split into small military states given to frequent wars with one another. During this "Indian medieval" period, the quality of art fell below the level of the Gupta empire achievements. There were several reasons for this, all of them adding up to a new way of life that had a lamentably stifling effect on the free, creative human spirit. The victory of Hinduism as the strongest Indian faith introduced the rigid socioreligious caste system dominated by the powerful Brahman priests, who composed the highest caste. Pomp and grandeur, elaborate ceremonies at which only the elite were permitted, royal greed, and superficial attention to meaningless detail contributed to spiritual decline. Yet all professed to be more fervently religious than ever, an interesting contradiction.

To clarify the history of this medieval period of dynastic conflict, the following chart may be consulted:

DYNASTIC CONFLICT

Palas	A.D. 730–1140
Pratiharas	mid-fifth century–mid-tenth century A.D.
Rashtrakutas	A.D. 753–974
Cholas	A.D. 846–1279
Senas	A.D. 1140–1280
Gangas	A.D. 496–1434
Chandellas	A.D. 831–1308
Solankis	mid-tenth century–A.D. 1299
Pandyas (Southern India)	mid-thirteenth century

MUSLIM PERIOD

The Delhi Sultans	1206–1526
The Moguls	1526–1857
Vijayanagara	1336–1565

The greatest artistic discovery of the age proved to be bronze casting. The final phase of Buddhist art evolved during this period, the Pala period, in the eighth through twelfth centuries A.D., and some sculptors in bronze produced statues of great beauty and refinement, like the figure of the bodhisattva Avalokitésvara in Plate 348.

Some medieval works of art were more directly influenced by the past than others. The twelfth-century male torso in Plate 349, while Indian in its dancelike posture, also bears traces of strong Greco-Roman influence. In the Bengalese stele, or pillar, in Plate 350, with its dominating figure of the god Vishnu, the boldness and solidity of the composition, the facial characteristics, and the finely chiseled detail provide a last glimpse of the classical Gupta tradition.

Compare this last stele with the Sena-period stele of a mother and child in Plate 351; while pretty enough in a rambling, decorative way, the Sena-period stele fails to make any emotional impact whatsoever. Consider, too, the compositional chaos of

348. **Figure of bronze bodhisattva Avalokitésvara (Pala period).**

349. **Male torso (twelfth century A.D.).**

167

a Hindu statue of the goddess Durga, slayer of the buffalo-monster Mahisha (Plate 352). This is a perfect example of the confused detail that weakened Indian art.

The same weakness can be seen in the Pratihara-period Buddhist statues of the eight-armed goddess Marichi (Plate 353) and the goddess Tara (Plate 354). Marichi, a dreadful divinity, is frequently represented with three faces, the most repulsive of which is a boar's snout. Her attendants generally include a band of animal-faced goddesses and Rahu, the demon of eclipses; they travel about together in a cart drawn by pigs. Tara, on the other hand, was known as the "Savior," "Giver of Favors," and was the feminine counterpart of Avalokitésvara, Lord of Compassion. In Plate 354 she is shown making her typical gesture of charity.

Durga was one of the goddess forms taken

350. **Bengalese stele with figure of Vishnu** (Pala-Sena period).

351. **Stele with mother and child from Gangarampur** (Sena period).

352. Durga, slayer of the demon
Mahisha (Pratihara period).

353. The eight-armed goddess
Marichi (Pratihara period).

354. The goddess Tara
(Pratihara period).

by Parvati, the wife and female counterpart of Siva. She was the daughter of the Himalaya, and variously appears in Hindu mythology as Uma the Gracious, Ambika the Mother, Sati the Good Wife, or Gauri the Shining and Golden One. Like Siva she has her fearsome or terrible sides as Durga the Unapproachable, Kali the Black, Bhairavi the Terrifying, or Karala the Horrific; as these she becomes the goddess of destruction. After destroying Mahisha, a buffalo-monster, she triumphantly danced upon its corpse; Plate 352 illustrates this guise. Her ten arms bristle with deadly devices: a harpoon, trident, sword, noose, bow, etc.

The Chola-period figures of Siva and Parvati indicate the full flowering of bronze sculpture under that dynasty. Three other bronze figures (Plates 355, 356, 357) further

indicate that, while contemporary stone sculpture grew increasingly stiff, metal images preserved more of the earlier Indian sculptors' graceful skill and vigor. These particular figures represent Vishnu and Siva. As cult images, they are designed to be seen from the front. Siva as "Lord of the Dance" became the principal theme of south Indian bronze sculpture. In Plate 357 he dances on the back of a dwarf that hostile sages have created out of a magic fire. From the dwarf's back rises a circular halo of fire that envelops the rhythmically moving limbs of the god. The crown on Siva's head touches the top of the halo, and his scarf flutters over its rims. It was believed that Siva would dance on the ruins of the earth after its destruction; following Siva's dance, Vishnu would go into his deep sleep so

356. Bronze statue of Siva (eleventh century).

357. Siva, "Lord of the Dance" (Chola period).

355. Bronze statue of Vishnu from Mysore (eleventh to twelfth centuries A.D.).

358. Ceiling of the Dilwara temple (eleventh century A.D.).

359. Interior of Jain temple, Mount Abu (eleventh century).

that he might bring forth the new world.

In Orissa and Gujarat, cities west of the Punjab region, the religious cult of Jainism flourished for centuries, and Mount Shu was one of its pilgrimage shrines. Jainism accepted the eternal existence of the individual soul and, over the years, had been supported by wealthy merchants and several kings. The multitudinous deities of Hinduism have no place in Jainism and therefore are rarely represented. Jain sculptors constantly repeated the same themes and created astonishingly fine patterns in carved marble that look as fragile as lace, as in the ceiling of the Jain Temple, Dilwara (Plate 358). The exteriors of this and other temples at Mount Abu are quite plain, in sharp contrast to their dizzyingly decorated main halls and painstakingly decorated pillars and arches (see Plate 359). The halls of each of these temples lead to a sanctuary with nine compartments, each with a figure of a Tirthankara, one of the twenty-four Jain world teachers; a compelling eleventh-century marble statue of one of them is shown in Plate 360. Certain examples of Orissa art seem to have closer ties to the rest of Indian art, however, and are more familiar to us.

A Hindu influence is felt in an intertwined snake god and goddess; and there is a Gupta flavor to the relief of a woman standing beneath a tree (Plates 361, 362). This last, as we have seen, is a frequent decorative theme in Indian art. It is based on a fanciful tale of a woman who was so beautiful that a tree burst into blossom at her touch.

360. **Marble statue of a Tirthankara, Mount Abu (eleventh century).**

361. Snake god and goddess from Orissa (tenth century A.D.).

362. *Woman under a Tree,* relief from Orissa.

As previously mentioned, royal greed and competitive self-importance went hand in hand with other medieval lapses in human values. Ornate palaces were built, but it is in temple architecture that we can see dynastic craving for grandeur and immortality in its extremes. Bearing witness to this are the Brihadishvara temple, Tanjore, of the Chola period (Plate 363) and the temple of Siva Nataraja, Chidambaram (Plate 364). The latter was built during the Pandya period in the middle of the thirteenth century when much greater importance was given to the architectural surroundings than to the temple itself.

The era of Moslem rule in India began when the Sultanate of Delhi was proclaimed in 1206. The Moslems had threatened the frontiers of India since the eighth century, and their fanatic zeal in spreading the faith of Islam was backed up by their greed for new territories. In the tenth century a Turkish Moslem kingdom arose in Ghazni in Afghanistan and became a constant danger to the northern provinces. The Indian states resisted Moslem advance until 1196, when the final conquest of northern India began. This resulted in the founding of the Sultanate of Delhi, with the Muhammed of Ghor as its first ruler. Central India and the Deccan desperately tried to withstand the invaders, but finally fell in 1292 and 1326, respectively.

The Moslems treated the Indians with arrogance and contempt, but the conflict of their cultures was eventually to produce a great art. The gulf between them was wide: Islamic buildings are basically strictly pro-

363. **Brihadishvara temple, Tanjore (Chola period).**

364. Temple of Siva Nataraja, Chidambaram (Pandya period, thirteenth century A.D.).

portioned masterpieces of bold engineering; Hindu architecture had been fantastic and extravagant, seeming to follow no logical form. Islamic sculpture is purely ornamental and abstract, since the Moslem religion forbade the making of human images. Conversely, Hindu sculpture is naturalistic, often erotic, delighting in all human, animal, and vegetable forms of life. Indian color, while sometimes glowing with the lovely orange-amber light of the Ajanta cave paintings, is essentially delicate, and its use in decoration is individual and irregular. Islamic color is brilliant and clear, and its use in decoration is geometric. As in China, calligraphy is used as an art and an important means of decoration.

Islamic architecture emerged from the marriage of Arab, Syrian, Byzantine, Persian, and, later, Turkish styles. In the Mediterranean area, its basic forms were the pillar, hall, and dome; in Iraq and Iran and, ultimately, in India, the brick vault and cupola were its most characteristic features. The first mosque in India, Quwwat-ul-Islam, made use of a colonnade surrounding a ruined Jain temple (see Plate 365). Nothing could be more different from the ornate but rather formless magnificence of the Hindu temples than the severe elegance of this building. The arches sweeping up to a point are termed "ogival" and are typical of Islamic architecture, as is the relief decoration in bands of geometric patterns and inscriptions. This sort of ogival arch and pilasters (square or rectangular pillars which project from a wall from top to bottom instead of standing free), rather than columns, domes, and cupolas, now began to appear in India. Another Jain temple, partly destroyed by Moslem armies during the

365. Ruins of the first mosque in India, Quwwat-ul-Islam.

366. Columns of Arhaidin-Ka-Jhompra mosque, Ajmer.

367. Detail from Arhaidin-Ka-Jhompra mosque, Ajmer.

invasions, was reconstructed as the Arhai-din-Ka-Jhompra mosque, located at Ajmer. Only part of the building survives today. Fortunately the splendid, soaring columns seen in Plate 366, which form part of the pillared nave, are still standing. The entrance and the structure surrounding it were built up in the original reconstruction from various other temples destroyed by the Moslems. By 1200 there was an abundance of Moslem artisans and craftsmen in India, and they used Islamic forms and ornament in rebuilding the temple as a mosque. Their native contributions are seen most clearly in Plate 367. The calligraphy carved in relief consists of texts from the Koran, the Moslem equivalent of the Bible; the carved decoration repeated in variations on the inner and outer walls includes, besides Arabic script, both geometric patterns and "arabesques," ornaments in which flowers, leaves, fruits—but no animate figures—are combined in a fanciful yet precise pattern.

The Moslem rulers' hold over their huge empire, however, was uncertain at best. Between 1348 and 1412 an internal rebellion and threats of foreign invasion split the empire into local sultanates, which often fought among themselves. In each of these provinces, local traditions influenced architectural styles. In Kashmir, Bengal, and Gugarat, the Hindu style of temple was used for Islamic purposes. In the Deccan the Bahmani sultans, warring relentlessly with neighboring Hindu kingdoms, strengthened their forces with Persian troops; consequently a Persian influence in Deccan architecture was noticeable as late as the end of the sixteenth century. Yet the Lodi sultans of Delhi (1451–1526) built mosques, tombs, and palaces in the classical Islamic style; the "Lodi Mosque" at Khairpur and the mausoleums of Sher Shah and Isa Khan are masterpieces of this style (see Plate 368).

The Moslem occupation of India influenced styles of painting in a much more positive way than it did those of architecture or sculpture, and we see in this period the birth of Indian miniature painting as a major art. Miniature painting began as decoration and illustration for both sacred and secular fourteenth-century manuscripts, and while the earliest miniatures show some distinctly Hindu details, they are originally Persian in form. The scenes are composed with great care and refinement, the drawing is flat, and physical movement seems to be frozen in mid-air. Facial expression is suggested only by the intensity of a character's gaze. The overall effect is one of stylized rhythm and great harmony.

368. **The mausoleum of Isa Khan, Delhi (1547).**

369. The monuments of Ranakpur (Hindu Renaissance, fifteenth century).

The most beautiful miniatures are those in the Rajput style of Rajasthan, in northern India. A religious and artistic revival started there in the fourteenth century, aided by a popular reform movement that swept away the idolatry and suffocating superstition of medieval Hinduism. Hindu resistance to the Moslems had a stimulating effect on all the arts and brought about in the late fourteenth century the "Hindu Renaissance" period. This in turn was later swept away by another mass movement which reinstalled Vishnu, in his incarnations as Krishna and Rama, as the fervently worshipped god of all-embracing love. These new ideas set off an explosion of sacred hymns and erotic songs, fresh and original art, epic tales and colorful stories, and supremely rich folk poetry.

With the coming of the Moguls, central Asian warriors who invaded India in 1526, a vast new empire was founded. To arrive at this, however, the Moguls were forced to make certain significant compromises. Indian Moslems refused to cooperate fully, thereby obliging the invaders to form an alliance with the aristocratic Rajputs of the north. With this alliance, the direction of Indian civilization was established for centuries to come—the result being a fascinating blend of Islamic and Hindu cultures.

Hindu culture, as has been noted, was revitalized in the late fourteenth century, and Hindu and Jain architecture experienced a renaissance which lasted nearly two centuries. The final flowering of an ancient style produced the monumental buildings at Ranakpur, Chittogark, and Mount Abu, to give a few examples. Many new temples were built along traditional lines, while existing ones were restored and copied. In Plate 369 we see the monuments of Ranakpur. Eighty forts and numerous temples were erected by order of Prince Kumbha of Mewar, including Jain temple on Mount Abu, Plate 370. The Hindu

370. Jain temple on Mount Abu (Hindu Renaissance, fifteenth century).

371. The temple of Minaksi at Madurai (sixteenth to seventeenth centuries).

Renaissance also reached to the extreme southeast of India, and the stupendous temples of Srirangram and Conjeeveram, with their magnificently carved groups of prancing horses, gods, goddesses, and warriors triumphing over their enemies, rose loftily into the sky.

The southern kingdom of Vijayanagar was the only Indian state that held off Moslem invasion for as long as three generations. But in 1565 its ruler was defeated by a grand alliance of all the Deccan sultans. True to the glorious artistic tradition of the south, the Vijayanagar kings had been great patrons and promoters of Indian art. Never had so many impressive and richly decorated temples, halls, and gateways been built; never had so many images and murals been cast and carved in bronze and stone. The style continued after the fall of the kingdom and inspired buildings like the temples of Minaksi, Chidambaram, and Rameshwaram (see Plates 371 through 373).

A carved pilaster from the temple of Minaksi at Madurai is shown in Plate 374. The female figure's dancelike position echoes

374. **Pilaster from the temple of Minaksi at Madurai** (sixteenth to seventeenth centuries).

375. **White marble Apsara (Hindu Renaissance).**

the grace of a white marble Apsara of the Hindu Renaissance (Plate 375). The Apsaras were represented in China as celestial musicians, but the original Apsaras were fertility goddesses transformed by early Indian Buddhists into heavenly beings who are often shown attending the Buddha.

The Mogul Empire was not firmly established until the time of Akbar the Great (1556–1605). An enlightened and generous ruler, he enlisted Hindus as well as Moslems for his ministries, married Hindu princesses, and permitted complete religious freedom. He beautified his capital, Delhi, with fairy-tale buildings set about with airy halls, flowering gardens, and restful fountains. One of the noblest monuments of the sixteenth century is Akbar's tomb at Sikandra (see Plate 376). Its arcades, screens of white and colored marble, pavilions, and turrets are set in a Persian garden; the tomb itself, which was once adorned with a priceless diamond, lies in a quiet court.

372.

Two views of corridors of the temple of Rameshwaram (eighteenth century).

373.

376. The tomb of Akbar at Sikandra
(sixteenth century).

378. Detail of the Red Fort, Delhi.

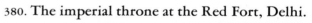

380. The imperial throne at the Red Fort, Delhi.

379. Doorway of gold and semiprecious stones,
the Red Fort, Delhi.

377. The Divan-i-Khas, or audience pavilion, at the Red Fort, Delhi.

Mogul palaces, such as the "Red Fort" at Delhi (Plates 377, 378), were supremely luxurious; they held bathing pools, music pavilions, little mosques, public and private halls, and such other splendors as an arched doorway actually made of gold and semiprecious stones (Plate 379) or a white marble throne inlaid with gold (Plate 380).

The Mogul emperors brought famous painters from the Persian court to teach the art of miniature painting to both Hindu and Moslem artists. Painters had begun to work in this form during the Hindu Renaissance, as previously mentioned; the earlier works bear a flat, patterned look, as seen in the illustrated leaves of a sacred Jain text, the *Kalpasūtra* (Plate 381).

Miniatures might illustrate religious mythology, historical works, epics, and romances or could be as straightforwardly decorative as some keenly observed and beautifully colored studies of birds (see Plate 382) or as reverent as the painting depicting the worship of Krishna in the "City of Gold" (Plate 383).

The Rajput paintings of the 17th to 19th centuries illustrate legends and myths of Krishna and Radha or Siva and Parvati,

381. Leaves from the *Kalpasutra* (Hindu Renaissance).

382. Studies of birds, by Miskina (late sixteenth century).

which appealed to all classes (see Plates 384, 385). The young Krishna, the cowherd god (an incarnation of Vishnu), charmed everyone with his beauty and magical flute playing. He chose a young girl, Radha, as his bride, and her passion for him symbolizes the soul's longing for God.

Mogul miniatures are among the most perfect of all Indian paintings, and in them Akbar saw his dream of uniting Islam and Hinduism partly fulfilled.

The applied arts of the Mogul period reached a greater perfection than ever before seen in India. Fabrics, particularly brocades; ceramics; and bronzes are equal to the best Persian works. Palace decoration was dazzling. Swords had hilts of jade or steel inlaid with gold and silver; cups were made of jade and crystal inlaid with gold and rubies.

383. *Worship of Krishna in the City of Gold* (*c.* 1600).

384. *Krishna and Radha* (Kangra school, late eighteenth century).

Clothes were of transparent white muslin or soft, brightly colored wool embroidered with small flowers made of gold thread. Enamel work and ivory carving were much appreciated; an especially fine sixteenth-century pendant representing the ten incarnations of Vishnu and a masterly carved eighteenth-century ivory plaque illustrating the marriage of Siva to Parvati are seen in Plates 386 and 387.

385. *The Toilette of Radha,* Rajput-Bahari school (eighteenth to nineteenth centuries).

386. Sixteenth-century enamel pendant.

387. Ivory plaque from Tanjore (eighteenth century).

But the jewel of the Mogul period, the achingly beautiful architectural paradise which the entire world associates with Indian artistic achievement, is the celebrated Taj Mahal (Plate 388). The Taj Mahal was built at Agra by Akbar's grandson, the heartbroken Shah Jahan, as the tomb for his legendarily lovely wife, Mumtaz Mahal. It took architects and masons from about 1630 until 1648 to complete the famous and complexly beautiful memorial, with its massive dome airily set off by minarets, fragile carved decorations, a reflecting pool, and perfectly balanced landscaping.

In the last period of Mogul rule applied art became more opulent, with elaborate ornaments and heavy gold and tinsel embroidery. By the end of the eighteenth century all that was great in the foreign Islamic culture had been completely digested by the Indian tradition, making Hindu and Islamic art almost indistinguishable.

All the natural splendor and variety of India has resulted in the development of a great civilization, in the birth and growth of religions, philosophies, and artistic styles, which together unquestionably represent one of the peaks of human achievement.

388. The Taj Mahal at Agra (*c.* 1630–1648).

CHINA

1. Map of China's principal historical centers.
2. Red earthenware jar from I-chou in Hopei, northeast China (c. 3000 B.C.). *Metropolitan Museum, New York.*
3. Painted earthenware jar from Pan-shan, Kansu (second millennium B.C.). *Musee Cernuschi, Paris.*
4. Painted earthenware vase from Ma-ch'ang, Kansu (1700-1300 B.C.). *Musee Guimet, Paris.*
5. Painted earthenware vase from Ma-ch'ang in Kansu, northwest China (c. 2000 B.C.). *Metropolitan Museum, New York.*
6. *Chia* type of bronze ritual vessel (Shang). *British Museum.*
7. *Chih* type of bronze ritual vessel (Shang). *Badalich Collection, Milan.*
8. *Chüeh* type of bronze ritual vessel (Shang). *Freer Gallery of Art, Washington.*
9. Covered *li* type of bronze ritual vessel (Shang). *Nelson Gallery of Art, Kansas City.*
10. *Tsun* type of bronze ritual vessel (Shang). *Metropolitan Museum, New York.*
11. *Fang-i* type of container with square cover (Shang). *Metropolitan Museum, New York.*
12. *Tsun* type of bronze ritual vessel with lid, in form of owl (Shang). *Victoria and Albert Museum, London.*
13. Bronze sacrificial cauldron of the three-legged *li* type (Shang). *Musée Guimet, Paris.*
14. *Yu* type bronze covered vessel with swing handle and *t'ao-t'ieh* mask of a tiger protecting a man or boy (Shang). *Musée Cernuschi, Paris.*
15. Bronze *ho* vessel with spout, lid, and *t'ao-t'ieh* mask (Shang). *Nezu Art Museum, Tokyo.*
16. Ritual dagger with jade blade and bronze handle, from An-yang (Shang). *Academy of Arts, Honolulu.*
17. Perforated green jade plaque (predynastic). *Academy of Arts, Honolulu.*
18. Jade *pi* disc (Chou). *Academy of Arts, Honolulu.*
19. Jade *ts'ung* from An-yang (Shang). *Academy of Arts, Honolulu.*
20. Bronze spiral finial with dragon's head (Chou). *Nelson Gallery of Art, Kansas City.*
21. Bronze *yu* with swing handle (Chou). *Metropolitan Museum, New York.*
22. Bronze vase of the *hu* type (Chou). *Nelson Gallery of Art, Kansas City.*
23. Ceremonial *chung* bell (Chou). *Nelson Gallery of Art, Kansas City.*
24. Bronze animal-shaped *tsun* (Chou). *Nezu Art Museum, Tokyo.*
25. Bronze *tsun*-type container in the form of a tiger (Chou). *Freer Gallery of Art, Washington.*
26. Bronze horse (Late Chou). *Nelson Gallery of Art, Kansas City.*
27. Bronze brazier with large and small dragons (Late Chou). *Metropolitan Museum, New York.*
28. Bronze *yu* with cover and swinging handle (Early Chou). *Fine Arts Museum, Boston.*
29. Bronze funerary figure of kneeling man (Chou). *Nelson Gallery of Art, Kansas City.*
30. Bronze statuette of little slave girl with jade doves (Late Chou). *Fine Arts Museum, Boston.*
31. Bronze acrobat with balancing bear (Chou). *Freer Gallery of Art, Washington.*
32. Painted wooden funerary figures (Late Chou). *Metropolitan Museum, New York.*
33. Preying bronze tiger (Art of Ordos, Late Chou). *Musée Cernuschi, Paris.*
34. Bronze ornament of animal combat (Art of Ordos). *Vannotti Collection, Lugano.*
35. Bronze scabbard (Art of Ordos, Han). *Musée Guimet, Paris.*
36. Bronze deer (Art of Ordos). *Musée Cernuschi, Paris.*
37. Elaborate jade *pi* disc (Late Chou). *Nelson Gallery of Art, Kansas City.*
38. Jade *pi* with dragons (Late Chou). *Nelson Gallery of Art, Kansas City.*
39. Jade fish and stag (Late Chou). *Metropolitan Museum, New York.*
40. Painted clay vase in form of owl (Chou). *Musée Cernuschi, Paris.*
41. Ceramic bowl with cover, of *tou* type (Chou). *Metropolitan Museum, New York.*
42. Pottery vase and cover with glass bead insets (Chou). *Nelson Gallery of Art, Kansas City.*
43. Brown-glazed stoneware bowl and lid (Chou). *Academy of Arts, Honolulu.*
44. Round box in lacquered wood (Chou).
45. Head of a beast in lacquered wood (Chou). *Academy of Arts, Honolulu.*
46. Bronze urn of the *tou* type (Chou). *Freer Gallery of Art, Washington.*
47. Bronze *hu*-type vase with inlay (Late Chou). *Vannotti Collection, Lugano.*
48. Pottery model of a house or watchtower from a tomb (Han). *Nelson Gallery of Art, Kansas City.*
49. Bronze table support (Late Chou or Warring States). *Nelson Gallery of Art, Kansas City.*
50. Gilt-bronze furniture support statuette of bear (Han).
51. Detail of a pottery tile from a tomb (Chou). *Nelson Gallery of Art, Kansas City.*
52. Funerary statue in gray pottery (Han). *Musée Cernuschi, Paris.*
53. Figurine of a woman carved in wood, adorned with glass and bronze (Late Chou or Early Han). *Honolulu Academy of Arts.*
54. Pottery statuette of a dancer (Han). *National Museum, Tokyo.*
55. Statuette of a female musician in painted terra-cotta (Han). *National Museum, Tokyo.*
56. Pottery tile depicting the meeting of Lao-tzŭ and Confucius (Han). *Musée Cernuschi, Paris.*
57. Gray pottery funerary tile of stag hunt (Han). *National Museum of Oriental Art, Rome.*
58. Painted pottery tile from tomb in Honan (Han). *Fine Arts Museum, Boston.*
59. Hill jar with stand in form of boy and beast (Han). *Nelson Gallery of Art, Kansas City.*
60. Lacquer box inlaid with silver (Han). *British Museum.*
61. Head of horse in green jade (Han). *Victoria and Albert Museum, London.*
62. Cave sanctuary at Tun-huang, Kansu (fifth century A.D.). *Photograph in the University of Kyōto.*
63. Detail of relief sculpture in dark gray marble from the cave temple of Lung-mên in Honan (Northern Wei). *Metropolitan Museum, New York.*
64. Bronze statue of seated Buddha Sākyāmuni (second half of fifth century A.D.). *Nelson Gallery of Art, Kansas City.*
65. Votive stele representing Buddha Sākyāmuni, in high relief against green leaf-shaped screen (Six Dynasties, sixth century A.D.). *Freer Museum of Art, Washington.*
66. Buddhist stele in terra-cotta (Northern Wei, sixth century A.D.). *Fine Arts Museum, Boston.*
67. Altarpiece in gilt bronze (524 A.D.). *Metropolitan Museum, New York.*
68. Pagoda of the Universe at Hangchow. *Photograph supplied by Kyōto University.*
69. Pottery horse (Northern Wei, c. 530 A.D.). *Freer Museum of Art, Washington.*
70. Jeweled bronze altarpiece (Sui, 593 A.D.). *Fine Arts Museum, Boston.*
71. Statue of bodhisattva (Sui). *Musée Cernuschi, Paris.*
72. Statue of bodhisattva Avalokitésvara in stone (Sui, late sixth century A.D.). *Fine Arts Museum, Boston.*
73. Figure of Buddha in painted stone (T'ang). *Metropolitan Museum, New York.*
74. Temple dedicated to the Buddha Vairocana, Lung-mên, Honan (T'ang). *Photograph from the Photograph Library of Kyōto University.*
75. Stone statue of the bodhisattva Avalokitésvara, or Kuan-yin (T'ang, eighth century). *National Museum, Tokyo.*
76. Ivory statuette of Kuan-yin, Chinese version of the bodhisattva Avalokitésvara (probably T'ang). *Metropolitan Museum, New York.*
77. Bronze sarcophagus supported by four guardians (T'ang, eighth century). *Freer Gallery of Art, Washington.*

78. Carved lokapala in painted wood from Tun-huang (T'ang). *Musée Guimet, Paris.*
79. Glazed pottery lion (T'ang). *Freer Gallery of Art, Washington.*
80. "Pilgrim flask" type of bottle in glazed earthenware (T'ang). *Victoria and Albert Museum, London.*
81. Glazed pottery camel (T'ang). *Nelson Gallery of Art, Kansas City.*
82. Statuette of lady playing polo, in unglazed pottery (T'ang). *British Museum, London.*
83. Figurine of dancing girl, in unglazed pottery (T'ang). *Nelson Gallery of Art, Kansas City.*
84. *Tuning the Lute and Drinking Tea,* hand scroll, ink and watercolor on paper, attributed to Chou Fang (T'ang). *Nelson Gallery of Art, Kansas City.*
85. *The Journey of the Emperor Ming-huang to Shu,* hanging scroll, ink and watercolor on silk (T'ang). *National Palace Museum, Peking.*
86. *Portrait of Fu Shêng,* hand scroll, ink and watercolor on silk (T'ang). *Municipal Museum, Osaka.*
87. *Deer in Autumn Landscape,* hanging scroll, ink and watercolor on silk (Five Dynasties). *National Palace Museum, Peking.*
88. *Listening to the Wind in the Pines,* hanging scroll, ink and watercolor on silk, by Ma Lin (dated 1246). *Palace Museum, T'ai-chung, Formosa.*
89. *Walking along a Mountain Path in Spring,* album painting, ink and light color on silk, by Ma Yüan (Sung). *Palace Museum, T'ai-chung, Formosa.*
90. *Waiting for Friends by the Light of Lanterns,* album painting, ink and watercolor on silk, by Ma Lin (Sung). *Palace Museum, T'ai-chung, Formosa.*
91. *Autumn in the Hills and River Valley,* hanging scroll, attributed to Emperor Hui-tsung (Sung). *Palace Museum, T'ai-chung, Formosa.*
92. *Landscape in Wind and Rain,* hanging scroll, watercolor on silk, attributed to Ma Yüan (Sung). *Seikado Foundation, Tokyo.*
93. *The Nine Dragons* (detail), ink and watercolor on paper, by Ch'en Jung (Sung). *Fine Arts Museum, Boston.*
94. *Tribute Bearers on Horseback,* hanging scroll, ink and watercolor on silk (twelfth century). *Metropolitan Museum, New York.*
95. *The Han Palaces,* album painting, ink and watercolor on silk, attributed to Chao Po-chu (twelfth century). *Palace Museum, T'ai-chung, Formosa.*
96. *The Traveling Peddler,* album painting, ink and light color on silk, signed by Li Sung (1210). *Palace Museum, T'ai-chung, Formosa.*
97. *The Poet Li Po,* hanging scroll, ink on paper, by Liang K'ai (mid-thirteenth century). *National Museum, Tokyo.*
98. *Portrait of the Ch'an Master Wu-Chün,* hanging scroll, ink and watercolor on silk (1238). *Tōfukukuji, Nara.*
99. *Sparrows Perching on Bamboo,* hanging scroll, ink and watercolor on paper, attributed to Mu-ch'i (mid-thirteenth century). *Nezu Museum, Tokyo.*
100. *Quail,* album leaf, color on silk, attributed to Li An-chung (twelfth century). *Nezu Museum, Tokyo.*
101. *Birds and Plum Blossom,* painting, attributed to Ma Lin (thirteenth century). *Goto Museum, Tokyo.*
102. *The Hundred Wild Geese,* section of a hand scroll, ink and color on paper, attributed to Ma Fên (twelfth century). *Academy of Arts, Honolulu.*
103. *Lotus Flowers and Water Bird,* hanging scroll, color on silk, by Te Ch'ien (Sung). *National Museum, Tokyo.*
104. Glazed pottery lohan (Sung).
105. Seated lohan, in dried lacquer (1099). *Academy of Arts, Honolulu.*
106. Head of a lohan, in dried lacquer (tenth to twelfth centuries). *Nelson Gallery of Art, Kansas City.*
107. Statue of bodhisattva in wood with traces of paint (Liao or Ch'in, during time of Sung dynasty). *Musée Guimet, Paris.*
108. Fragment of a fresco showing bodhisattva Kuan-yin (twelfth century). *Academy of Arts, Honolulu.*
109. Statue of bodhisattva Kuan-yin in lacquered and painted clay (Liao or Ch'in dynasty, during time of Sung Dynasty). *Nelson Gallery of Art, Kansas City.*
110. Bodhisattva Avalokitésvara or Kuan-yin (twelfth century). *Fine Arts Museum, Boston.*
111. Jade vessel in the form of a bronze *kuei* (Sung, thirteenth to fourteenth centuries). *Academy of Arts, Honolulu.*
112. Green jade plaque (Sung). *Musée Guimet, Paris.*
113. Animal-shaped vessel in proto porcelain (Six Dynasties). *Metropolitan Museum, New York.*
114. Greek-influenced white porcelain vase (T'ang). *National Museum, Tokyo.*
115. *Ting* bowl, white porcelain with transparent glaze (Sung). *Metropolitan Museum, New York.*
116. Glazed ceramic vase of *Tz'ŭ-chou* type (Sung). *Metropolitan Museum, New York.*
117. Glazed ceramic "bottle vase" (Sung). *Musée Guimet, Paris.*
118. *Chien* ware jar (Sung). *Academy of Arts, Honolulu.*
119. *Chün* cup with light blue glaze (Sung). *Victoria and Albert Museum, London.*
120. *Chün* ceramic jar with blue and purple glaze (Sung). *Victoria and Albert Museum, London.*
121. *Chün* flowerpot vase with mottled blue and red glaze (Sung). *Metropolitan Museum, New York.*
122. *Bamboo* (detail), from an album by Wu Chên (Yüan, 1280–1354). *National Palace Museum, Peking.*
123. *Bamboo and Chrysanthemums,* hanging scroll, ink on paper, signed by K'o Chiu-ssu (Yüan, 1290–1343). *Palace Museum, T'ai-chung, Formosa.*
124. *Autumn Colors in the Ch'iao and Hua Mountains,* from a hand scroll, ink and light colors on paper, signed by Chao Mêng-fu (Yüan, 1254–1322). *National Palace Museum, Peking.*
125. *Boating on the River in Autumn,* hand scroll, signed by Shêng Mou (Yüan). *Palace Museum, T'ai-chung, Formosa.*
126. *Dwellings in the Hills in Autumn,* hanging scroll, ink and colors on paper, signed by Wang Mêng (Yüan). *Palace Museum, T'ai-chung, Formosa.*
127. *Mountain Scenery with a Little House on the River,* hanging scroll, ink on paper, signed by Ni Tsan (Yüan). *Palace Museum, T'ai-chung, Formosa.*
128. *The Patriarch Pu-tai,* hand scroll, ink on paper, signed by Yin T'o-lo (Yüan). *Nezu Museum, Tokyo.*
129. *Seated Lohan,* hanging scroll, colors on silk, attributed to anonymous Buddhist painter (Yüan). *National Museum, Tokyo.*
130. *Landscape,* hanging scroll, ink and colors on silk, signed by Sun Chün-tsê (Yüan). *Seikado Foundation, Tokyo.*
131. Statue of Kuan-yin in painted wood (Yüan). *Metropolitan Museum, New York.*
132. Statue of Kuan-yin in painted wood (Yüan). *Metropolitan Museum, New York.*
133. Statue of Kuan-yin in painted and gilded wood (Yüan). *Nelson Gallery of Art, Kansas City.*
134. Rosette-shaped silver plate (Yüan). *Nelson Gallery of Art, Kansas City.*
135. Blue-and-white pottery vase (Yüan). *Metropolitan Museum, New York.*
136. Headrest in *chün* ware (Yüan). *Metropolitan Museum, New York.*
137. Gate of Supreme Harmony, Forbidden City, Peking (Ch'ing).
138. The Imperial Summer Palace outside Peking (Ch'ing).
139. The Imperial Summer Palace outside Peking (Ch'ing).
140. *Returning Home at Evening in Spring,* hanging scroll, ink and colors on silk, by Tai Chin (Ming). *Palace Museum, T'ai-chung, Formosa.*
141. *Walking with a Stick,* hanging scroll, ink on paper, by Shên Chou (Ming, 1427–1509). *Palace Museum, T'ai-chung, Formosa.*
142. *Landscape,* hanging scroll, ink on paper, by Shên Chou (Ming). *Academy of Arts, Honolulu.*
143. *The Farewell,* hanging scroll, ink and colors on paper, by Wen Chêng-ming (Ming). *Vannotti Collection, Lugano.*
144. *Landscape with Rocks and Mountains,* hanging scroll, ink and light colors on paper, signed by Lu Chih (Ming). *Vannotti Collection, Lugano.*
145. *Fishing in the River in Autumn,* hand scroll, ink and colors on silk, by T'ang Yin (Ming). *Palace Museum, T'ai-chung, Formosa.*

146. Fan with chrysanthemums and bamboo, ink and colors on paper, by T'ang Yin (Ming). *Vannotti Collection, Lugano.*
147. *Saying Farewell at Hsün-yang,* hand scroll, ink and colors on paper, by Ch'iu Ying (Ming). *Nelson Gallery of Art, Kansas City.*
148. *Waiting for the Ferry in Autumn,* hanging scroll, ink and colors on silk, marked with the seal of Ch'iu Ying (Ming). *Palace Museum, T'ai-chung, Formosa.*
149. *Mountain Valley,* hanging scroll, ink on paper, by Ku Itze (1628). *Metropolitan Museum, New York.*
150. *Mountain Landscape,* album painting, ink and colors on paper, Tung Ch'i-ch'ang (Late Ming). *Vannotti Collection, Lugano.*
151. Illustration for the poem "The Homecoming," hand scroll, ink and light colors on silk, by Ch'ên Hung-shou (Ming). *Academy of Arts, Honolulu.*
152. Traveling chest in red-lacquered wood (Ming, 1613). *Musée Guimet, Paris.*
153. Cabinet in black-lacquered wood inlaid with mother-of-pearl and gold lacquer (Ch'ing, early eighteenth century). *Musée Guimet, Paris.*
154. Lacquered cabinet with raised decoration in gold (Late Ming or Early Ch'ing). *Musée Guimet, Paris.*
155. Incense burner in carved lacquer with jade top (Ming). *Victoria and Albert Museum, London.*
156. Figurine of Kuan-yin in wood (Ming). *Metropolitan Museum, New York.*
157. *Mei-p'ing* porcelain vase (Ming). *Musée Guimet, Paris.*
158. Blue-and-white porcelain vase with gentlemen playing checkers (Ming). *Victoria and Albert Museum, London.*
159. Pilgrim flask in porcelain (Ming). *Victoria and Albert Museum, London.*
160. Glazed porcelain vase decorated with enamel (Ming). *Freer Gallery of Art, Washington.*
161. Porcelain stem-cup (Ming). *Palace Museum, T'ai-chung, Formosa.*
162. Porcelain dish in five colors (Ming). *Private Collection, Rome.*
163. *Landscape,* hanging scroll, ink on paper, by Wang Shih-min (Early Ch'ing). *Vannotti Collection, Lugano.*
164. *Mountain Landscape,* hanging scroll, ink and colors on paper, by Wang Chien (Ch'ing). *Freer Gallery of Art, Washington.*
165. *Landscape with Mountains and Forests,* ink and colors on paper, by Wang Hui (Ch'ing). *Academy of Arts, Honolulu.*
166. *Landscape in the Style of Tung Ch'i-ch'ang,* hanging scroll, ink and colors on paper, by Wang Yüan-ch'i (Ch'ing). *Vannotti Collection, Lugano.*
167. *Landscape in the Style of Ni Tsan,* hanging scroll, ink on paper, by Wu Li (Ch'ing). *Vannotti Collection, Lugano.*
168. *River Landscape,* hand scroll, ink on paper, by Kung Hsien (Ch'ing). *Nelson Gallery of Art, Kansas City.*
169. *The Coming of Autumn,* hanging scroll, ink on paper, by Hung-jên (Ch'ing). *Academy of Arts, Honolulu.*
170. *River Landscape,* album painting, ink and colors on silk, by Chu-ta (Ch'ing). *Academy of Arts, Honolulu.*
171. *Mountain Landscape,* album painting, ink and colors on silk, by Chu-ta (Ch'ing). *Academy of Arts, Honolulu.*
172. Porcelain ginger jar with cover (Ch'ing). *Metropolitan Museum, New York.*
173. *Famille verte* porcelain *rouleau* vase (Ch'ing). *Metropolitan Museum, New York.*
174. *Famille noire* porcelain vase with overglaze enamel painting (Ch'ing). *Nelson Gallery of Art, Kansas City.*
175. Miniature porcelain vase (Ch'ing). *Metropolitan Museum, New York.*
176. Blanc de chine statue of Kuan-yin (Ch'ing). *Campilli Collection, Rome.*
177. "Dog of Fo," *famille verte* porcelain statuette (Ch'ing). *Nelson Gallery of Art, Kansas City.*
178. Cupboard in lacquered wood (Ch'ing). *Nelson Gallery of Art, Kansas City.*
179. Throne of Emperor Ch'ien-lung, in carved red lacquer inlaid with gold (Ch'ing). *Victoria and Albert Museum, London.*

KOREA

180. Map showing chief cultural centers of Korea.

181. Gold belt buckle, probably of Chinese workmanship (second century B.C.). *National Museum of Korea, Seoul.*
182. The Buddha Amitābha, Northern Wei Buddhist sculpture, gilt bronze (577 A.D.). *Tonghyun Kim Collection.*
183. Terra-cotta tomb slad (seventh century A.D.). *National Museum of Korea, Seoul.*
184. Vessel in form of warrior on horseback, fired clay (Early Silla). *National Museum of Korea, Seoul.*
185. Gray pottery ritual oil lamp (fifth or sixth century A.D.). *National Museum of Korea, Seoul.*
186. Fragment of terra-cotta relief showing lokapala attended by lion (Great Silla, seventh century A.D.). *National Museum of Korea, Seoul.*
187. Funeral urn in glazed stoneware (Great Silla, eighth to ninth centuries A.D.). *Freer Gallery of Art, Washington.*
188. Gilt-bronze statue of the Buddha Maitreya (seventh century A.D.). *Fine Arts Museum, Duksoo Palace.*
189. Wooden statue of Yokasa Youra, the bodhisattva of healing (eighth to ninth centuries A.D.). *National Museum of Denmark.*
190. Gilt-bronze statue of Bhaisajyaguru, Master of Medicine (eighth to ninth centuries A.D.). *National Museum of Korea, Seoul.*
191. Melon-shaped celadon pitcher (eleventh to twelfth centuries A.D.). *Academy of Arts, Honolulu.*
192. Flask in painted celadon ware (eleventh to twelfth centuries A.D.). *Academy of Arts, Honolulu.*
193. Shallow celadon bowl, inlaid with lotus flower and aster pattern (twelfth century A.D.). *Freer Gallery of Art, Washington.*
194. Celadon vase of *mei-p'ing* type, inlaid with "Thousand Cranes" design. *Hyung-pil Chun Collection.*
195. Yi wine jar in white porcelain with underglaze painting of vine leaves and grapes (seventeenth to eighteenth centuries A.D.). *Museum of the Women's University of Ewha.*
196. *Portrait of a Monk,* colors on silk (Yi, fourteenth century A.D.). *British Museum, London.*
197. *Landscape in Rain,* hanging scroll, ink and colors on paper, by Hyônjae Sim Sajong (eighteenth century).
198. *Rocks in the Sea,* hanging scroll by Tanwôn Kim Hong-do (eighteenth century). *Hyung-pil Chun Collection.*
199. *Concert on the River,* album painting, ink and colors on paper, by Hyewôn Sin Yun-bok (eighteenth century). *Hyung-pil Chun Collection.*
200. Hanging scroll depicting tiger, ink and colors on paper, by Hyônjae Sim Sajong (eighteenth century). *National Museum of Korea, Seoul.*

JAPAN

201. Map showing chief cultural centers of Japan.
202. Statuette in pottery (Jōmon). *National Museum, Tokyo.*
203. Statuette in pottery (Jōmon). *National Museum, Tokyo.*
204. Statuette in pottery (Jōmon). *National Museum, Tokyo.*
205. Statuette in pottery (Jōmon). *National Museum, Tokyo.*
206. *Haniwa* hen in clay (fifth to sixth centuries A.D.). *National Museum, Tokyo.*
207. *Haniwa* horse (Yayoi). *National Museum, Tokyo.*
208. *Haniwa* monkey in clay (fifth to sixth centuries A.D.). *National Museum, Tokyo.*
209. *Haniwa* warrior with helmet, pottery (Yayoi). *National Museum, Tokyo.*
210. *Haniwa* figure of a man, pottery (Yayoi). *National Museum, Tokyo.*
211. *Haniwa* woman in decorated dress, pottery (Yayoi). *National Museum, Tokyo.*
212. Kondō Hōryūji near Nara (seventh century).
213. Pagoda of Hōryūji near Nara (seventh century).
214. Detail of a gilt-bronze "banner" (Asuka). *National Museum, Tokyo.*
215. Carved statue of Kudara Kwannon, camphorwood (seventh century).
216. Carved statue of Miroku, pine wood (Asuka).

INDIA

INDEX